The Law of the Seed

A short story by

Ron E. Schmidt

Bradenton, Florida

THE LAW OF THE SEED
By Ron E. Schmidt

www.TheLawOfTheSeed.com

Copyright © 2011 by Ron E. Schmidt
All rights reserved.

The Law of the Seed story is a work of fiction. The characters, incidents, and dialogues are products of the author's imagination and are not to be construed as real. Any resemblance to actual events or persons, living or dead, is entirely coincidental.

This book or parts thereof may not be reproduced in any form, stored in a retrieval system, or transmitted in any form or by any means electronic, mechanical, photocopy, recording, or otherwise without express written permission of the author, except as provided by United States of America copyright law.

The material in this electronic publication can be stored only on one computer at one time and is intended for use by the purchaser. You may not forward, copy, or transfer the publication or part thereof, whether in electronic or in printed format to another person or entity.

All scripture quotations, unless otherwise indicated, are taken from the *Holy Bible, New International Version* ®. NIV®. Copyright © 1973, 1978, 1984 by International Bible Society

Published by Outcome Publishing
9607 State Road 70 East
Bradenton, Florida 34202
www.outcomeministries.com
(941) 920-0355

Printed in the United States of American

What others are saying about *The Law of the Seed*.

"Both my husband and I have read this book and we decided that we are definitely ready to follow The Harvest Principle and The Law of the Seed. We are excited to start our planning this weekend. Not only did we learn a lot from reading this book but we thoroughly enjoyed the story and wish we could spend a weekend at Ripple Farms to meet all of the Financial Farmers."
—Robin P.

"I wanted to tell you that your book is really good and very informative. It was written in very simple verbage every one can understand. The principles were orchestrated in a manner that I have never read before. I have known about planting seeds and reaping but never in a story which relates to all of us. Most of us have been at least once in situations where things were so tight that you could almost give up on life. All of us and anyone who reads it especially in these times will be able to use those principles accordingly."
—Norma Y.

"This book really taught me how to put things in the proper perspective. The principles are time tested over and over again and yet we seem to wander from their basic teachings. We can apply the Law of the Seed to almost every aspect of our lives.....finances, family, relationships and our future. Reading this book will instill a call to action in each of us."
—Wes T.

A simple, yet compelling story, that, if applied in these difficult economic times, will make a huge difference not only in peoples' financial lives but by being blessed by sharing with others. May we all be a part of the "ripple" to make a difference in our world one stone at a time.
—Rita R.

"After reading this book, it was easy to see that it is the work of someone with a servant's heart. God has definitely used your spiritual gifts and experience to create a story line that will attract people from all walks of life. Regardless of a person's level of financial experience, The Law of the Seed is a book that has a very pleasant way of addressing the uncomfortable topic of personal finance. Thank you for putting your heart into this work for all of us."
—Chuck S.

"Law of the Seed…straight forward and engaging revelations of how and when to plant your seeds to maximize your harvest in a community of financial farmers."
—Bayne B.

"I found the book ideal for today's economic situation. The Harvest Principle makes perfect sense! With a little planning and preparing, we too can be Financial Farmers."
—Helen R.

"I read the book in one sitting. I thought it was great and it was a page turner. I sat up until almost midnight reading it after church. It was not too long and it wasn't too short. I know that sounds like something Goldilocks would say but if a book is too long you sometimes get bored and don't finish it. It did leave me wondering what was in the packet that Jim and Jenny got at the farm?"
—Angela D.

I have read several books on finance and investing. I would describe most of them as dry. Have you ever read a chapter, then skipped to the center to see if it gets any better? I don't think that will happen today. This book was easy to read because Ron laid it all out in a story about regular people. No super heroes, no vampires. Take care of your "SEED" and you will live better next month.
—Dana M.

This book is dedicated to you, the future Successful Financial Farmer. May you discover the wisdom of *The Law of the Seed* to achieve real and lasting financial success.

Acknowledgments

I want to say thank you to:

My parents for planting the seeds of truth in my life;

*My wife, Kim, for her constant support,
patience and love;*

My kids, Heather and Caleb, who bring joy to my life;

*Ray, Linda and Bruce for putting up with me
as their big brother and for their support;*

*Wes Thompson, who has been my
encourager and good friend;*

*Dana and Tamia Mills, for their
input and encouragement;*

*Tom and Holly McAndrew, for their
creative spirit and insight;*

*To my Lord and Savior, Jesus Christ,
for through him all things are possible.*

Contents

Introduction 1
   1. Overwhelmed 3
   2. The Ripple 7
   3. Seed of Hope 13
   4. Ripple Farms 25
   5. Imagine 31
   6. The Garden Plan 38
   7. The Preparation 48
   8. Taking Action 59
   9. Putting the Pieces Together 69
   10. Farmer's Truths 78
   11. It Takes Water 96
   12. The Challenge Trail 116
   13. To Protect 122
   14. Truth of Forgiveness 131
   15. The Harvest Celebration 138
   16. The Bridge 149
   17. The Ripple Effect 156
A Final Word… 160
Appendix 162

Introduction

Imagine a life of no debt. No car payments. No credit card bills. And ... no mortgage! How would you feel? Would your life be different? You bet it would!

Just think what you could do with an extra $400 per month because you don't have a car payment. Or imagine an extra $1,800 because you no longer have a house payment. With the extra money would you purchase a rental property? Start a business? Fund your retirement so that you could retire sooner? Have your spouse quit work and stay home? Give more to your church or a favorite charity? What would you do?

My goal in writing this book is to help you achieve that lifestyle. The Law of the Seed is a system based on 5 foundational principles that will lead you from a life of stress and worry to peace and hope for a better financial future.

You will find as you read this book that it's not your typical financial book. Instead you will discover an engaging and entertaining story of a couple who find answers to their financial troubles in the most unlikely place–a farm.

Follow Jim and Jenny from their home where everyday financial struggles overwhelm them to a weekend adventure where they learn new principles that will change their life and yours.

The Law Of The Seed

1
Overwhelmed

Almost any man knows how to earn money, but not one in a million knows how to spend it.
Henry David Thoreau
181-1862, American Essayist, Poet, Naturalist

Economy is half the battle of life. It is not so hard to earn money as to spend it well.
Charles Haddon Spurgeon
1834-1892, British Baptist Minister

"I'm sorry Darlin' but this card is not working either," the elderly Wal-Mart cashier reported back in a sweet Southern accent, handing the credit card back to Jenny.

Embarrassed, Jenny fumbled through her purse for another credit card. She could hardly believe that her first two cards did not work. *Were the cards damaged? Or were they maxed out?* It didn't matter now; she just needed to find another card to pay for her $19.87 grocery bill.

After a few seconds, which seemed like minutes to Jenny, she found another credit card, a brand new VISA card.

"Here try this one."

Taking the card, the white-haired cashier carefully slid it through the register. Nothing. Then again, the words "declined" flashed across the register.

Overwhelmed

"I'm sorry but we can't use this card either. It seems that the credit card company is not accepting it." Trying to be helpful, and in a grand-motherly type fashion, the cashier leaned over and said, "You know we accept personal checks. Perhaps you could…."

The cashier's words drifted off. Tears began to form in Jenny's eyes as she took the card back and tried to find some money in her purse.

"Mommy I have to go to the bathroom," pleaded five year old Jordan.

Every eye was on her; the cashier, the people behind her, and even her two kids. She could feel the people staring at her.

"Here you go," a man in khakis shorts and a white shirt said as he handed a twenty dollar bill to the cashier. Don't worry I'll take care of this one.

"No…please I really don't need your money. I'm fine. I am just having problems with my cards. I think it's just a banking problem. We have money. I just don't have any cash on me and I left the checkbook at home by mistake."

"Don't worry. I'm sure you have some money. Let me just pay for this so that you and your kids can be on your way," he said re-assuredly.

"I can't accept your money. I do not even know you."

"Look, here is my card. It has my name, address and phone number on it. After you get this sorted out, you can pay me back if you like. No rush."

Jenny looked at the man. He seemed genuine enough and very sincere. "Alright, I will send you the money as soon as I get home. Thank you. I…I mean we really appreciate it."

The cashier handed the change back to the man.

The Law Of The Seed

Jenny, a little stunned but grateful, grabbed the grocery bag and placed it in the cart behind two year old Megan who was drinking a juicy bottle, completely unaware of what was happening.

Pushing the grocery cart with Jordan in tow, Jenny exited the store and made her way back to her car. With the kids securely fastened in their car seats, she started the car and headed back home. Tears of embarrassment and frustration began to freely fall down her cheeks.

I cannot go on like this, she thought to herself. *Something has to change.*

* * * * *

"Mr. Smith, this is Norma from the front desk, I have a call for you on line three from a Mr. Young."

"Thank you Norma. Did he say who he was with?" asked Jim who was busily working on an Excel spreadsheet for a client.

"No he didn't Mr. Smith. Do you want me to find out?"

"No, that's alright Norma. I'll go ahead and take it."

"Hello, this is Jim Smith, how can I help you?"

"Mr. Smith my name is Mr. Young and I am with Deitwiller and Shuster. Your account with Dr. Rowe Dentistry has been turned over to us to collect. We expect full payment in the amount of $1,378.25 today. I can process a credit card payment or a check payment over the phone now. Which payment method will you be using today?"

"You have got to be kidding. I don't have the money. If I did, I would have paid Dr. Rowe months ago! And why are you calling me at work?"

Overwhelmed

"Calm down Mr. Smith. I am calling you at work because you and your wife have not been returning my calls to your house. Dr. Rowe is entitled to be paid for his services."

"But I don't have the money! I told Dr. Rowe over a month ago that we were struggling financially and that I would pay once we were back on our feet. Doesn't he remember our conversation?"

"Mr. Smith, I'm not sure about your conversation with the doctor's office. All I know is that your account is 120 days delinquent and we have been hired to collect," said Mr. Young.

"Listen I do not have time for this, especially while I am at work. I have to go." With that, Jim slammed the handset down and hung up the phone. Leaning back in his office chair Jim slowly rubbed his head, as if to rub away the conversation from his memory.

"Something has got to change," he muttered to himself, "or else I am going to lose it."

Jim left work early. He just wanted to get away and think. After an hour of driving around town aimlessly, he found himself pulling into his driveway. Not ready to face his wife yet, Jim just sat in his car, thinking of what he was going to do. What was he going to tell Jenny? He had no answers.

2
The Ripple

Do more than belong: participate.
Do more than care: help.
Do more than believe: practice.
Do more than be fair: be kind.
Do more than forgive: forget.
Do more than dream: work.
William Arthur Ward
1921-1994, an American Writer

If you can imagine it, you can achieve it.
If you can dream it, you can become it.
William Arthur Ward
1921-1994, an American Writer

"The phone has been ringing off of the hook," reported Linda. "I have received over twenty requests for more information on the camp just this morning alone."

"And I have received another nine paid registrations from the web site over the weekend," Joe responded as he printed them off.

"This is awesome! At this rate our camp will be filled up by this weekend," responded Linda.

"Folks, this is exciting but at the same time it's sad to know that so many people are hurting. But like I said when we first started this camp, 'build it and they will come'," reminded Ray, the group's elected Camp Director.

The Ripple

"Well they're coming," responded Joe enthusiastically.

"Pizzas are here!" Hank announced as he entered the room with his wife, Sue, and their long time friends Roger and Carolyn Thomas.

"Everyone ready?" Hank asked. Before anyone could respond, he answered his own question. "Good. Let's get started. Roger, would you mind blessing the food and our meeting?"

"Be happy to" responded Roger. "Lord, thank you for this day…"

For over five years, the four couples had been meeting regularly at the home of Hank and Sue Taylor, who owned a large farm just outside of town. The weekly routine involved having lunch together, reading a short devotion, which was followed up by a short discussion and then closing with prayer. Forty five minutes. That was the routine.

Hank was the oldest member of the group having reached the big "five-o". He was a degreed civil engineer, who gave up his career to pursue real estate investing after he grew bored with his job. Together with Sue, his wife and mother of their two children, Heather and Caleb, they developed a large portfolio of rental properties. It was during their early investment years that they met Roger and Carolyn Thomas.

Roger and Carolyn were semi-retired general contractors who had two kids, Chase and Hunter that were similar in age to Hank and Sue's kids. The couples hit it off when they were introduced to each other by an acquaintance at a Chamber of Commerce event.

Over time, the two couples became best of friends and business partners, investing in various new home construction projects and rehabs. Eventually the two became neighbors when they acquired a large farm and an adjoining property through a bank foreclosure.

The Law Of The Seed

Through their small group study at church, the Taylor and Thomas families became good friends with Ray and Cindy Cunniff and Joe and Linda Redden; each with a unique story.

Early in their marriage, Ray and Cindy Cunniff were missionaries in Germany. After serving for a number of years, they returned to the States where Ray accepted a job for a non-profit company that provides high-tech medical equipment to third world countries. Cindy, once an elementary school teacher, is a stay-at-home mom and full-time home school teacher to their four adopted kids.

Joe and Linda Redden were the youngest members of the small group. After experiencing the death of their newborn daughter and Joe losing an executive position in a bank, both within a month, the pair returned to church to find comfort and support.

During those years the group grew close. They cried together over the loss of a baby, the news of an unexpected death and loss of a job. There were also times that they laughed and celebrated together. The group was close.

It was a year ago that Hank felt that the group had reached a plateau. Hank believed that he along with his six close friends and wife were no longer growing deeper spiritually or socially. He wanted to challenge them, to stretch them. The event, which the group would fondly refer to as the "ripple", took place on a Friday morning in January. It was on that cool morning that things changed.

On that particular morning the group was asked by Hank to meet him at the barn at 7:00 sharp. They did. Hank did not say a word but motioned for everyone to follow him. Through the fence, across the pasture they followed Hank. No one said a word as they made their way through the large oak trees that lined Hank's 550 acre farm. After about ten

The Ripple

minutes of steady walking, Hank finally stopped at the edge of a large pond. Eight chairs waited for them.

"Take a seat everyone," directed Hank softly.

Hank walked behind the chairs as he waited for them to take their seats. "Friends, take a look at the pond. Focus on the center. What do you see?"

After a minute, Sue broke the silence, "Honey, I see nothing. There are no fish jumping, no ducks, the pond looks like glass."

It was at that moment that Hank threw a rock. It hit near the middle of the pond. The splash startled the group.

"Now, tell me what do you see?"

"A splash," Joe responded.

"No. What else do you see? What did the splash cause? Look close."

"Ripples. I see ripples," the group shouted in unison.

"Good. That is what I see also." Hank having the group's attention continued, "Friends, for the last couple of months I've really been convicted about us. I want our group to do more. To make a splash with our lives that will ripple across and affect those that we come in contact with, our pond. I want our group to make a difference."

Hank walked over to the empty chair and sat down. Looking over at his wife and then at his friend, "Is it just me that feels this way? Or do you feel the same and want to make a splash that impacts people's lives?"

It was Roger who made the first move, walking over to the edge of the pond; he found a rock and threw it into the water. Turning around he addressed the group, "I want my life to count. I want to make a splash. Hank I'm with ya."

It didn't take long for everyone to find a rock and throw it into the pond. They were all on board and committed to making a difference.

The Law Of The Seed

The group was energized. Over the next couple of weeks they met twice a week, brainstorming about ways to cause a ripple. It was Linda and Sue that came up with the "splash" one evening while the group was relaxing around a small outdoor fire that Hank and Roger had started.

Linda, the owner of a successful accounting firm, started the conversation while gazing into the fire. "People are struggling financially. I see it every day. People call me and want to know what I can do to help. I try, but…"

"You know, Linda, that's it," Sue interrupted. "People with financial problems—they're our pond. As you were talking it reminded me of how many more people Hank and I are counseling at church that have financial issues compared to a couple of years ago."

"Sue, that is exactly what I was thinking," Linda blurted out, excited that they were on to something.

"Great minds think alike," replied Sue with a smile. They both laughed.

Joe, seeing the opportunity continued, "The economy is down, foreclosures are up, bankruptcies are climbing, people are hurting. Linda and Sue, you're right! That is our pond. And our splash and ripple are…?"

"Our ripple is the positive effects of teaching common sense finances with those we come in contact with," answered Ray, his eyes transfixed on the fire.

The group nodded in agreement. The fire crackled and roared to life as Roger added another dry piece of wood.

Ray's wife, Cindy, who was generally cautious, joined the conversation. "There are so many people teaching finances these days. Some are great and can be heard on TV and radio and others are all hype. What will make us different? What will make people take notice?"

The Ripple

Roger, who was uncharacteristically quiet, spoke up. "It's this farm."

"Huh?" was the general response from everyone.

"Let me finish. We could teach people how to be farmers—financial farmers. Planting, growing a garden, weeding and harvesting, can all be tied to personal and family finances. The splash is financial farming and the ripples produced are the positive results, the changes that people will experience when they learn farming. Let's teach people how to be financial farmers." Roger repeated himself to add emphasis.

"I love it Roger," responded Carolyn with a gentle kiss on his cheek.

The Law of the Seed was born.

3
Seed of Hope

*An anxious heart weighs a man down,
but a kind word cheers him up.*
Proverbs 12:25 NIV

*Hope is the thing with feathers, that perches in the soul,
and sings the tune without words, and never stops at all.*
Emily Dickinson
1830-1886, American Poet

Jenny watched Jim slowly emerge from the car. He looked beaten and worn down. Sitting on the couch in front of the family room window, Jenny followed her husband's slow steps.

Jim still didn't know what to say. He had no answers. All he could do was pray and to ask for help. He felt like he had failed. Walking up the sidewalk, he saw Jenny watching him through the window. He tried to smile.

All Jenny saw was hopelessness in his expression. She got up and stood by the couch as Jim opened the front door. Before he could place his briefcase down Jenny asked, "Jim, are you alright?"

Jim looked up. Emotions began to well up inside of him. Tears began to form in his eyes. He looked at Jenny and saw that her eyes were all red. "Not really. How about you? Have you been crying?"

Jenny rushed to her husband hugging him and then began to sob. "Jim, I cannot go on like this. Something has to change."

Jim could no longer control his emotions. Embracing his wife, he began to cry. Whispering in her ear, "I agree. Something has to change."

It wasn't until the kids were put to bed that Jenny was finally able to talk to Jim. Jenny found him sitting at the kitchen counter rummaging through the stack of mail.

"Jim do you have some time to talk?" she asked cautiously.

"Sure, now is a good time." Jim pushed the mail aside and turned toward his wife.

Grabbing one of the bar stools, she pulled up alongside of him. "Jim, today the kids and I were shopping at Wal-Mart. I just ran in to get a few things that we were out of, milk, a few bananas, some bread, and some lunch meat. It wasn't very much. The total came to less than $20. When I tried to pay, none of the credit cards worked. I had no cash and I left the check book on the counter this morning while I was paying bills. But I know there was no money in there either."

"So you left the store?"

"I was going to, but a man that was standing behind me paid the bill."

"Did you know him?"

"No."

"Let me get this straight. A perfect stranger just decided to be nice and pay for groceries," Jim shook his head. "Did he want something in return?" Jim asked skeptically.

"No Jim! He was being genuinely nice," Jenny snapped defensively. "He told me that we didn't have to pay him back but that if we wanted to we could. And then he handed

The Law Of The Seed

me his business card. Here take a look at it." Jenny slid the card over to Jim.

Jim, sensing his wife's frustration, "Jenny, I'm sorry. I just don't know why a stranger would be willing to pay someone's grocery bill. It just sounds strange."

Jim picked up the card. Looking it over he noticed that it wasn't your average business card. On the front of the card was written, "The Law of the Seed – How to Become a Successful Financial Farmer." The bottom left was written "The Ripple Group – Members Roger & Carolyn Thomas." Turning over the card Jim read the following, "Sharing Proven Principles for Successful Financial Living. Visit us at www.TheLawoftheSeed.com."

Jenny followed Jim's eyes as he read the card. "I checked out the web site. It's very interesting. This is something that I would like us to do. But you need to take a look yourself." Standing up, she continued, "I'm going to go get the laptop so that you can check it out."

Jenny returned quickly with the web site already up. "Here, take a look."

Knowing that it might be a late night, Jenny asked, "Can I make you some coffee?"

"Sure, that sounds good," Jim responded as he pulled the laptop closer to him.

The web site opened up to a video where questions flashed across the screen;

Is MONEY a problem?
No MONEY for bills?
Facing foreclosure?
Late on payments? Using credit cards to pay for bills?
Creditors calling you?
Stressed? Frustrated? Lost hope?
Because of No MONEY

Ripple Farms

*Discover Financial Freedom
At Ripple Farms and learn about
The Harvest Principle and The Law of the Seed
Become a Successful Financial Farmer
And Experience
True Financial Freedom*

Jenny watched Jim from the kitchen. His skeptical face, which she had seen many times over their 10 years of marriage, turned to curious. She watched him click through the web pages.

Pouring the fresh brewed coffee into Jim's favorite coffee cup and topping it off with some French vanilla creamer, Jenny delivered it to him, along with some dessert she had made earlier.

"Honey, what do you think?"

Jim just shook his head from side to side and slowly replied "I cannot believe this…"

Surprised by Jim's reply, Jenny shot back before Jim finished, "What do you mean you cannot believe this?"

"Jenny, just let me finish," his voice sounding a little bit tense. "What I wanted to say is that I cannot believe this is happening. For the last couple of months, I have been trying to think of a way to get us out of this financial mess. But I don't know what to do. Then today I received a call from a collection agency trying to collect full payment for that root canal work that I had done last summer. I lost it. I just left the office and drove around, thinking of what I can do to get us out of this."

Turning to Jenny, "Honey, I don't know what to do but I believe this retreat can help us. We need to do this!"

The Law Of The Seed

Overcome with joy and a sense of relief that Jim was willing to do this she kissed him and whispered, "thank you."

*   *   *   *   *

Roger stepped out of the house on to the front porch. It was a gorgeous Saturday morning. A pair of pigeons were rummaging around the front lawn. Off in the distance a woodpecker was heard tapping one of the large oak trees. Another set of birds were calling to each other. There was a slight breeze and the air smelled clean.

He began scanning the front yard for the morning's paper. Muttering to himself, "now where did the paper boy throw that paper? Well... I'll be." Roger was pleasantly surprised that the paper landed right on the step, not more than two feet in front of him. Careful not to spill his favorite morning gourmet coffee he reached down and picked up the paper.

Roger was reading the local section of the paper on the porch swing when his wife, Carolyn, joined him. "Dear, I printed an email out for you. I think it's from the family that you told me about—the one that you helped at Wal-Mart."

Roger folded the paper in half and placed it on the porch railing in front of him and took the email from Carolyn.

"Dear Roger, I want to say "thank you" for helping my wife out yesterday at Wal-Mart. Jenny and I would like to personally repay the $20 you loaned her. We also have some questions about 'The Law of the Seed' and your farmer program. Jenny, the kids and I have nothing planned for tomorrow and we were hoping that we could meet you somewhere. You can call (555-7273) or email us back.

*Grateful,
Jim and Jenny Smith."*

* * * *

Jenny woke up to the sound of the phone ringing. *What time is it?* She thought as she rolled over in bed. 9:40 a.m. the clock read. Pulling the covers away, she sat up and placed her feet on the floor. In the distance she could faintly hear Jim talking and the kids watching morning cartoons. *Boy, it felt good to sleep in a little. I knew I was worn out.*

She had just finished brushing her teeth when she heard Jim enter the bedroom calling her name. "Jen, are you up?" Seeing that she was already getting ready, "Did you sleep well?"

"I sure did. Thanks Honey, for letting me sleep in and for keeping the kids quiet."

"Not a problem. You needed it." Changing topics Jim asked, "Guess who just called?"

"I don't know. Someone from work?"

"No, try again."

"My parents?"

"Not even close. I'll give you a hint. You shop at the same place."

Sensing Jim's enthusiasm for this little question and answer game, Jenny responded playfully, "Okay, what place is that, Thompson Jewelers or Bed Bath and Beyond?"

"No, the grocery store."

"Well that narrows it." Jenny emerged from the bathroom. Looking at Jim, "Alright you win, I give up. Now who was it?"

"It was Roger, the guy that paid for your groceries yesterday."

The Law Of The Seed

"Really?"

Jim nodded.

Jenny went over to the bed to begin making it. Straightening out the covers, "How did he get our number?"

"I emailed him last night. And I told him that we wanted to pay him back personally and that we wanted to find out a little more about the seed program."

"So what did he say?"

"He said that he and his wife are free this afternoon and he invited us to the farm."

"The farm?"

"Yes, the farm that we saw on their web page."

"The farm, boy, the kids are going to love that! What time are we supposed to be there?"

"One o'clock."

Jenny quickly replayed the things that she had planned to do today in her mind; laundry, cleaning the kid's room, and washing her car. All of her to—do items could wait. This was more important.

"That will be perfect," she responded excitedly. "I'm looking forward to meeting them."

* * * * *

The thirty minute drive to Roger and Carolyn's home went by quickly. Their home was located just outside of the city limits on the East side. Pulling onto the driveway the Smith family was greeted by a pair of large oak trees on either side of the drive. A freshly painted white fence lined the drive up to the house.

The house looked warm and inviting, featuring a large wrap-around porch with four porch swings, one on either side of the house and two on the front porch. Leading from the driveway to the wide staircase was a brick path lined with colorful blooming annuals.

"Jim, this place is beautiful," Jenny said as she started to help Jordan out of the car.

Jim already had little Megan in his arms and walked around to where Jenny was. "Jen you're right, this place is beautiful."

"Good afternoon fellow Wal-Mart shopper," Roger said with a wide grin as he and Carolyn walked down from the porch. Extending his hand to Jim, "It is good to meet you. I'm Roger and this is my wife, Carolyn."

"Good to meet you two and thank you for inviting us over," responded Jim.

Jenny still caught up with the canopy oak trees, the white fence and the country home, "I just love your place here. It is absolutely beautiful."

"Thank you Jenny," responded Carolyn. "God has really blessed us."

Squatting down to little Jordan's level, Carolyn asked, "And who do we have here?"

Jordan responded in a quiet shy voice, "Jordan Smith."

"Why that is a nice name. Jordan, I am so glad that you came today. And who is that?" Carolyn pointed to Megan.

"That's my sister, Megan. She's two."

"Come up to the porch and let's sit awhile and talk," invited Roger.

The group made their way up to the porch where, to the delight of Jordan and Megan, toys were laid out on a blanket. No instruction was needed. The two raced over to the blanket and began to play quietly. As they did, the two couples sat down on a pair of porch swings that overlooked the front yard and began to talk.

The Law Of The Seed

For the next hour Jim and Jenny shared their financial struggles with Roger and Carolyn, at times blaming each other for their money problems. They felt completely at ease sharing all this with Roger and Carolyn, who had made them feel at home and just like one of their family.

After Jim and Jenny had described their financial situation, Roger responded. "I'm so glad that you shared with us. Times are tough and believe me, Carolyn and I can relate to the situation that you two are in because we faced similar hardship when we first got married. But we overcame it and so can you."

Carolyn, still sensing some resentment from Jenny that had surfaced during the conversation, spoke up. "It was tough at first. I blamed Roger for our problems–like you Jenny. But after some wise advice, deep soul searching and reflection, I realized that I was to blame also."

Carolyn reached across to the next swing, and touched Jenny's hand. "By not saying anything when Jim was making those purchases, you were condoning his actions." Carolyn continued to look at Jenny as she shook her head in disagreement.

"When you guys took out the home equity loan, didn't you co-sign?" Jenny didn't need to respond, Carolyn already knew the answer. "Do you see you have some responsibility in this and that makes you partially to blame?" Jenny lowered her head.

"Now listen carefully Jenny…Jim, you too. Both Roger and I discovered early on that blaming each other would not solve our problems; it would only make them worse. One of the first things that we did was to forgive each other. Forgiveness heals—and it allowed us to move on."

Jenny looked up, "You're right, Carolyn. I guess it was just easy for me to blame Jim rather than accept some of the responsibility. And I do need to forgive."

The sound of a golf cart interrupted the conversation. Everyone turned toward the direction of the noise. Driving through the oak trees were four kids on a gas powered six-seat golf cart.

"Don't kids have the perfect timing?" Roger said sarcastically. Turning to Jim and Jenny, "two of those kids are ours and the other two…"

"Hi Mom. Hi Dad," shouted Chase and Hunter.

"Hi Mr. Roger and Ms. Carolyn," shouted Heather and Caleb in unison.

Pulling up to the porch, the four kids exited the golf cart and jumped their way to the front porch.

"Kids, I want you to say hi and introduce yourselves to our new friends, Mr. Jim and Ms. Jenny and their kids, Jordan and Megan."

Heather, the oldest of group at thirteen stepped forward and held her hand out. "Hi I'm Heather, the daughter of Hank and Sue Taylor; we live next door."

"And I'm Caleb, Heather's brother and protector," replied Caleb with a smirk as he stepped up to Jenny. Caleb was eleven.

Joining Heather and Caleb, Hunter, the youngest at ten stepped in front of his older brother, "I'm Hunter and…"

"And I'm Chase, as you probably already figured out, we are the kids of Roger and Carolyn."

"Great to meet you all," responded Jim. "So what are you four up to?"

"Oh we are just working on a little business idea that we all came up with," responded Heather.

The Law Of The Seed

"Yah, all of our parents challenged us to grow our seeds by starting a business this summer when school gets out," interjected Hunter.

"We're going to make our own splash," replied Caleb.

Grabbing Hunter and Caleb by the arms, Chase called out to his business partners, "Come on guys, we have got to get going." Looking at Jim and Jenny, "It was really nice meeting you. But you have to excuse us; we have a lot to do."

Through the front door and up the stairs the kids went. You could hear them taunting each other all the way up the stairs about who was going to make it up first.

Jenny turning to Carolyn commented, "Your boys are wonderful and your neighbor's kids too. Even starting a business...I'm impressed."

"Thanks Jenny, we are very proud of them. But like all kids, they have their moments."

Roger rose out of his porch swing, "I know that you probably have other things you have to do today, but before you leave we wanted to introduce you to our neighbors, Hank and Sue Taylor. They are Heather and Caleb's parents and good friends of ours. We teach the Law of the Seed program at their place. It will just take another 30 minutes or so. Do you have a few more minutes to meet them and talk about the program?"

"Of course we do. That is one of the reasons that we came to see you—and that reminds me..." Jim reached in his pocket and handed Roger an envelope that contained a thank you card and a $20 bill. "Here's a little card and the $20 we owe you."

Roger tried to hand the card back but was stopped by Jenny. "Roger your willingness to help shows what kind of person you are. Please accept our repayment so that you can help someone else again."

"Well alright then. Carolyn and I will use the money to help someone else. Now, are you ready to head over to see the farm?"

As soon as the word "farm" was mentioned Jordan jumped up and down excitedly. "Take me, take me," he yelled.

The group all climbed into the golf cart and off they went to see the farm and to meet Hank and Sue.

* * * * *

Jenny could not go to sleep. She kept replaying the events of the day in her mind. "Jim?" she whispered, hoping that Jim was still awake.

Jim was also just lying in bed staring at the shadows on the ceiling. "Yah."

"Thank you for making today possible and for agreeing to go next weekend. I know that it's going to help us." Jenny paused for a moment and then rolled over, "I love you."

Jim turned his head toward Jenny and gently kissed her. "I love you too. And I'm looking forward to next weekend. We really could use a break." Jim turned his head back towards the ceiling and closed his eyes. *Please Lord, let this retreat be our answer,* he prayed silently.

The Law Of The Seed

4
Ripple Farms

*Listen to advice and accept instruction,
and in the end you will be wise.*
Proverbs 19:20

*It takes a great man to give sound advice tactfully, but a
greater to accept it graciously.*
Logan P. Smith
1865-1946, Writer

Jim and Jenny arrived a few minutes before 6 p.m. at the farm. There were around twenty cars and trucks parked in what appeared to be a fenced-in pasture. Registration signs directed them along the side of a large red barn to a pair of horse stables. A sign directly atop the wooden entrance read "Registration and Lodging".

They were greeted by a young lady dressed in blue jean coveralls with a red handkerchief around her neck and a straw hat that freely dangled from behind her head. "Welcome to Ripple Farms, I'm Heather and I'm here to check you in to your stall."

"Heather, it's good to see you again, you look all grown up. We met you last weekend at Roger and Carolyn's place. We're Jim and Jenny Smith," replied Jim.

"I knew you looked familiar. Well, I am so glad that you decided to join us. I know that you will enjoy your weekend with us." Heather looked through the registration box and pulled out a yellow sheet. "It looks like you will be staying in stall Sea Biscuit, which is the fourth stall on the left. Here is your key."

"One more thing that I need to tell you about is the Gathering Bell. When you hear the sound of the bell, it means it's time to gather in the barn. That is where we eat and hold most of our meetings."

"Mr. Jim and Ms. Jenny, I'm glad that you came. Enjoy your stay."

Jim and Jenny left the registration desk and walked toward their room. They were completely amazed. The front of the rooms actually looked like stalls. Each stall had photos of famous horses; Man-a-war, Seattle Slew, Spectacular Bid and many others. Opening their door they found a nice cozy room which contained a small bathroom, queen size bed with a pair of end tables and lamps, a couch, a desk with a computer and printer, and a coffee table that contained a pair of straw hats and a box labeled "Financial Farming Kit". Both of them were pleasantly surprised with their accommodations. Soon after unpacking their clothes, the Gathering Bell sounded.

Stepping outside their stall, they joined a group heading to the barn. Some of the couples appeared to be in their mid-40's and 50's and there were a few others that looked like newlyweds. Once they reached the barn, they were directed to the center, where three rows of tables awaited them. Each one decorated with a checkered red and white table cloth, place settings, which included colorful cups, a lantern, and baskets full of seeds.

"Good evening everyone. If you can make your way to your seats we will get started," came a man's voice from the speakers.

"On behalf of the entire Ripple Farms' staff, I would like to welcome you here tonight. I'm Farmer Ray, your camp

The Law Of The Seed

director. I'm especially excited for you because I know that you will not leave here the same person as you arrived. Your life will be changed. For the next three days you will learn the Harvest Principle and the Law of the Seed by working on the farm."

"Well, I could go on but I have to admit the smell coming from the kitchen is making me hungry. So let me go ahead and pray for our meal and our weekend. Then I will share a little more after dinner."

A prayer was said and then dinner was served. For all of the guests, especially Jim and Jenny, this was no ordinary meal. Food was brought out on large platters and placed in the center of the tables. On each platter were large portions of corn, baked potatoes, chicken and steak. Each table was expected to pass around the food and everyone was to take what they wanted. The food was delicious.

Jim and Jenny shared their table with two other couples and a single mother. The conversations began with introductions then quickly led to why each of them were there. All had similar stories of hardship. Jim and Jenny were not alone.

Everyone was nearly done eating their meal when Camp Director Ray made his way to the microphone on stage. "Well, wasn't that good?" The group responded with applause. "Believe it or not, all of the food that you ate tonight was grown on this farm by other financial farmers just like you. And you will have the same opportunity to grow this very food this weekend."

"Well, now I need some volunteers. Actually..." Ray said with a wide grin that spread across his face, "I have already drafted some of you to help clear the tables. Everyone who was drinking out of a red cup, well... you are our bus-boys and gals tonight." You could hear laughter

Ripple Farms

spread across the various tables as each person was identified. At Jim and Jenny's table, a man by the name of Maurice was the one. He was a good natured person who hammed up busboy duties by addressing everyone as "Sir and Maam" and by re-arranging the dessert forks and spoons.

After a few minutes Ray interrupted the clean up by stating that everyone who had the yellow cups was required to go to the kitchen and deliver the dessert, fresh-baked apple pie. This time it was Jenny's turn. Jim loved every minute of it, teasing her about the quality of service and promising her a huge tip because she was cute.

After about 10 minutes the lights in the barn grew dim and a video on either side of the stage began playing. The video started by showing dollar amounts that scrolled from top to bottom on the big screens; $296,450, $32,000, $22,200, $12,600, $7,800, $3,700, $3,150, $1,780, $700, $650, $335, $220. "$381,585 total debt. That was what we owed." A couple appeared on the video. They looked to be in their early 50s. They introduced themselves as Hank and Sue Taylor. They went on to share their story about the financial struggles early on in their marriage. Hank admitted it was him that brought most of the debt to their marriage. The video showed photos of their kids, vacations, and their ranch called the Taylor Ranch ... and then it abruptly ended.

The lights above the stage turned on and lit up Hank and Sue Taylor. "Folks," Hank started off in a slow deep voice, "That was fifteen years ago. Today the Taylor Ranch is called Ripple Farms."

Applause erupted when the group realized that Ripple Farms was the very place where they were.

After the applause subsided Sue continued, "We turned our lives of debt and financial stress around by applying

The Law Of The Seed

principles that we learned. This weekend we want to share those principles with all of you. We call them financial farming principles through our Law of the Seed program. I can promise you that if you take to heart and apply what you learn this weekend, your financial lives will be transformed." As soon as Sue spoke those words, a proverb appeared on the video screen: *Listen to advice and accept instruction, and in the end you will be wise.*

Hank moved forward and placed his arm around Sue's shoulder. "Folks, Sue is right. If you listen, then accept what you've heard, and then apply it to your lives; you will be a successful farmer. Take a look at the screen and watch four couples whose lives have been transformed."

The video was very emotional. For close to 25 minutes the couples shared their financial struggles: credit card debt, home in foreclosure, verge of divorce, job loss, car repossessed, stress, feelings of failure. Most of the couples and individuals present could identify with one person or another. The video was a prelude to the first lesson for the couples.

The lights came up and joining Hank and Sue on stage was Ray. Ray stepped up to the microphone. "Powerful video wasn't it? How many of you can identify yourself with one of these four couples?" Hands rose all over the barn.

"In just a minute I am going to dismiss you to your room. In the next 47 minutes I need you to fill out the form entitled 'The Weeds Worksheet'. You can find this in the notebook binder which is located in the kit you received. Write down every debt you owe. Write down the lender and the amount. Total it up and then record the amounts on the front of the Weeds envelope and meet me, along with the rest of the Financial Farm team, at the bon fire. "

"Got it? Any questions? Good. We will see you in 47 minutes at the bon fire."

The group quietly exited the barn. Jim and Jenny went to their room. Jenny went straight to the box and opened it up. Inside was a book, a 3-ring binder, a notepad, envelopes, some pens, seed, and a calculator. Jenny grabbed the notepad and sat at the small coffee table. "Jim, you ready."

Jim was rummaging through his briefcase. "Almost, I'm trying to find the debt list that I made up last night. I had a feeling that we would need this."

"Honey, I am so proud of you for being prepared."

"I found it. You ready to record these numbers?"

"I'm ready."

Jim read off their laundry list of debt. It included school and furniture loans, gas cards, credit card debt, car and boat loans, home mortgage and a personal loan from Jenny's parents. The total was $238,160 of which $198,735 was for the mortgage and the rest of the $37,425 was just debt. Jenny filled out the worksheet and Jim filled out the envelope. Just as they had finished, the Gathering Bell sounded.

5
Imagine

If you can dream it, you can do it. Always remember this whole thing was started by a mouse.
Walt Disney
1901-1966, American Artist, Film Producer

The Harvest Principle
The seed is the future. Take care of the seed and the seed will take care of you.

The bon fire was located about 100 yards from the stables in an open field. Around the fire were large benches that were hewn out of oak trees. Each bench held six people comfortably. At the entrance to the bon fire was a large carved sign that read, "Imagine Circle".

Jim and Jenny were the first to arrive.

"Jim and Jenny," called Carolyn as she rose from her seat. "Why don't you two sit next to Roger and me?"

"We'd love to," Jenny responded eagerly.

Once Jenny was comfortably seated, Carolyn leaned closer, "So what do you think, Jenny?"

"This place is beautiful. I love what you all did to the stables making them into rooms. And the barn–what a great idea. You know, Carolyn, I think the best experience for me so far was the video testimonies. One of the couples on the video I could so easily relate to."

"I'm glad to hear that you are enjoying the experience, Jenny." Carolyn scooted forward in her seat and leaned forward to look at Jim who was sitting on the other side of Jenny. "Jim what do you think?"

"I have to agree with Jenny, this place is nice. It was more than I expected. Even the dinner was nice. But I am still wondering how this is all going to help us with our money situation."

Jenny elbowed Jim in the ribs.

Carolyn saw Jim flinch from Jenny's elbow. "Jim, the night is still young. I guarantee that we will be able to help with your financial situation. You just need to be patient," she said with a warm smile.

Just then another couple arrived. Soon the entire group was seated around the fire.

Ray and his wife, Cindy, stood up. Ray began, "Welcome to the Imagine Circle. Tonight will be like no other that you have ever experienced. Each person that has participated in the Imagine Fire has sat where you are sitting now and has left a changed person. I know that when you leave here tonight, you will leave changed."

"At dinner you heard Hank and Sue tell their story, their money story. In just a few minutes you are going to hear some more money stories from the rest of the team. My wife, Cindy, is going to tell you our story, and then Joe and Linda will share their story, followed by Roger and Carolyn." Ray looked at his wife, "Babe, go ahead and tell our story."

"Ray and I started our lives together as missionaries in Germany. Our salary wasn't the greatest but we managed. After a few years we moved back to the States to start our family. We soon found out that we were unable to have any children of our own, so we adopted. We ended up adopting four kids, two boys and two girls. Ray took another job working for a non-profit organization that requires him to fly around to different parts of the world so he is not home all the time. I quit my job as an elementary teacher to take care of our kids."

"Our finances were tight. Non-profits do not pay the best, so we adjusted. Despite having only one income, we are almost debt free. No car payments, no credit card debt, nothing. All we owe is on our house. We did this by applying the Law of the Seed to our lives."

"Thank you Babe." Ray hugged us wife. "Next, I would like you to hear from Joe and Linda."

Linda stood up from her seat, "Joe and I have been very foolish with our finances. Early on in our careers we made some dumb mistakes. Joe was a vice president for a large bank and I owned my own accounting firm. We had great incomes, a nice home, expensive cars, a boat, and every electronic gadget that a guy could want. Even though we had a lot of income, we typically saw our savings account not growing. We were great at telling other people what to do with their finances, but we did not follow our own advice. We had book knowledge but we lacked the heart knowledge. It wasn't until we applied the Law of the Seed that we finally and truly understood real peace in our personal finances."

Roger and Carolyn stood up. "Friends, I believe that things happen for a reason, whether good or bad," Carolyn began.

"Years ago when I had my two boys, I decided to leave the corporate world and raise our two children. Roger and I believed that we could easily survive on Roger's salary. Roger was a real estate broker and developer. We were blessed. Like Linda and Joe, we got caught up in the 'stuffitus' disease. We had the nice clothes, the cars, and the house. We traveled. It was great until the housing market collapsed. Our income dropped by three quarters. The problem was that I could not accept that. I lived like we were still making as much money as before. But it caught up to us." Carolyn's voice cracked. She glanced at Roger.

Roger placed his arm around Carolyn and continued for Carolyn, "It did catch up to us. We lost our vacation home, creditors called and harassed us, and we even contacted our attorney to begin filing for bankruptcy. But before we filed, some good friends shared with us the Law of the Seed. Today, Carolyn and I can stand before you and state that not only did we pay back every creditor, but we are living a life completely debt free. No monthly car payments, no mortgage, and no credit card debt."

Applause and cheers irrupted.

Hank and Sue joined Roger and Carolyn. Hank spoke. "Tonight you heard all of us share our financial lives with you. And everyone spoke of the Law of the Seed and how it transformed our lives. The first step that we took began by assessing where we were financially. We all filled out the Weed Form just like you did this evening."

"The listing of each weed showed us what was choking our financial seed from growing. The debt—the weeds that you listed and that are contained in the envelope you are holding, is robbing you and your family of a bountiful harvest."

Hank walked around the bon fire, pausing at each bench, making sure to look at everyone.

"This place we call the Imagine Circle. The reason that we call it that is because it is in this place that we imagine a life of being debt free and having an abundance. Wow, can you believe a life with no debt?" Hank paused for a moment to let the words sink in.

"Tonight, I want you to share. I'm going to have you come up as a couple, one couple at a time, and share with us your monthly debt payment. And then I want you to share what you would do with that money if you no longer had to make those payments. I'm also going to have you share your total debt with Sue so that she can record it. Then I want you to throw the envelope in the fire to simulate your debt going away. Burning the weeds, so to speak."

"Who wants to go first?"

Directly across from Jim and Jenny, a man rose with his wife. He was a handsome muscular man and his wife was petite and pretty. As they neared the front to where Hank and Sue were waiting, the glow of the fire highlighted their faces. Although they were in their mid-thirties, life's financial stresses had made them appear to be much older.

Clutching each other's hand, they made their way to the front. The man shared with Sue their total debt and then he cleared his throat by making a small coughing sound and raised his head. "I...I... can't even imagine being debt free," he stammered.

"I really can't," tears began to roll down his cheeks. "For over ten years now, I have borrowed from banks, friends and family to support my business. I owe more than $575,000 to them. I don't even have money to buy the kids birthday presents. As a father and husband, I've let my entire family down...and..." He began to sob.

There was a brief moment of silence; only the crackling of the fire could be heard as a piece of wood fell deeper into the fire. "I know what we would do," his wife still clinging to his hand replied. "We would give a portion of our income to organizations like yours that help people to not get into trouble like us."

With that she took the envelope from her husband's hand, crumpled it up into a tight ball, and threw it into the fire. They both stood for a moment gazing into the fire as the flames consumed the ball of debt, and then they made their way back to their seat.

Looking around the bon fire there was not a dry eye. Everyone was moved. Everyone could relate to the stress of being in debt. A slow minute passed with not a sound being made. It was Jenny who made the next move. She reached for Jim's hand and gently squeezed it and stood up.

They made their way to the front and were met by Sue. Jim shared the total debt amount with Sue and then turned to the group.

"We were kind of surprised at our monthly debt payments which are around $3,056. Having no debt would mean that we could start saving for our kids' college and more for retirement," Jim responded.

"And it also means that you don't have to work as hard and can spend more time at home," replied Jenny.

One by one all the couples made their way to the Imagine Fire and shared their story and then tossed their envelope into the fire.

"Folks," Hank began in a solemn voice. "Debt is not fun. Owing money to others when you have no money, is stressful. That stress affects lives, relationships and it affects our health."

"Each one of you shared what you would do with the 'extra' money once you were debt free. We Financial Farmers, call that the Harvest Principle. You see when a farmer plants a seed he is not just planting a seed. In his eyes he is planting a future. He knows that if he takes care of that one seed, in the end it will take care of him by yielding a fruit or a vegetable. But if he takes care of all of the seeds, it will produce a crop and he will have a great harvest. That will allow him to take care of his family and the families of many others."

The Law Of The Seed

"The Harvest Principle is a principle for life. You see, the seed can be a job, a relationship, or even finances. You are here today because you did not take care of the financial seed. As a result, your harvest has been limited or non-existent and you are now experiencing the pain of that harvest."

Those words stung Jim.

Hank continued, "Before we leave tonight let me encourage you by saying, 'It is not too late.' Despite what you may think or even feel. It is not too late to learn the Harvest Principle and apply the Law of the Seed and gain control of your lives. Tomorrow we will begin sharing the Law of the Seed."

"Well, it's getting late and we have a long exciting day ahead of us tomorrow, so let's call it a night. My advice to you is to go straight to bed because we will rise early in the morning. Also, as you leave, the staff has something to give you to remember our little talk this evening. See you in the morning."

As the group left the imagine circle they were handed a packet of seeds with the words *"The Harvest Principle"* written across the top and then the words *"The seed is the future. Take care of the seed and the seed will take care of you,"* written directly underneath it.

Jenny took the small packet of seeds and read it and then passed it on to Jim. "Honey, I am so glad that we came. Are you?"

Jim placed the seed packet in his pant pocket and then took Jenny's hand and gently squeezed it. Replying in almost a whisper, "Of course I am, this is exactly what I needed."

6
The Garden Plan

Always have a plan, and believe in it.
Nothing happens by accident.
Chuck Knox
1932—Present, Coach

Plans fail for lack of counsel,
but with many advisors they succeed.
Proverbs 15:22

It was 5:10 a.m. when Jim and Jenny woke to the clear sound of a rooster crowing. Jenny tried to muffle the morning wake-up call by hiding her head under the pillow. *Just a few more minutes of sleep,* she thought.

Jim, an early riser, jumped out of bed and headed straight to the bathroom to shave. He wanted to get ready quickly so that he would have some time to look through the workbook.

After a short ten minutes the rooster crowed again. This time it was followed up by a woman's voice, "good morning farmers, rise and shine. Today is shaping up to be a great day. The weatherman says that it will be clear and sunny. We need everyone to dress for some physical farm work and to report to the barn in 30 minutes. See you in shortly."

Jenny rolled over in bed and looked at the clock, 5:20. Muttering to herself as she sat up in bed, "I did not sign up for this."

The Law Of The Seed

Jim, stepping out from the bathroom caught only part of what Jenny had said, "Jen, sorry I didn't catch what you said."

"It was nothing." Jenny rose from the bed and slowly made her way to the bathroom.

"I wonder what they have in store for us this morning? It seems pretty early." Jim commented as he flipped through the pages of the notebook.

"Morning? It's still night outside! I can't remember the last time that I got up before six."

Jim hearing the tone in Jenny's voice tried to defuse the conversation. "You know, Jen, I'm pretty sure that they have something special planned. So far everything they have done has been unique."

Jenny didn't respond. *A nice hot shower will wake me up,* Jenny thought as she stepped into the shower.

Jim and Jenny joined the rest of the group in front of the barn. It was still dark outside and there was a slight chill to the air. Roger and Carolyn exited from the barn.

"Good morning farmers," exclaimed Roger. "This morning Carolyn and I have something very special that we want to show you and share with you."

"Yes we do," continued Carolyn, "before we share, we have some fresh-brewed coffee, hot tea, hot cocoa and warm apple cider inside. Please make yourself a cup and then join us up in the hay loft, which is directly above the dining area. There are stairs by the kitchen that will take you there. See you in a few minutes."

Jenny was glad that they offered hot chocolate since she was not a coffee drinker. The richness of the drink woke her up. It was exactly what she needed to warm her body and awaken her senses.

The Garden Plan

Roger and Carolyn were standing at one end of the hay loft in front of a large opening. In front of them were a couple of rows of hay bales.

"Please grab a seat," directed Roger pointing to the hay bales.

Carolyn began, "last night at the Imagine Circle each of you shared about your financial situation. You wrote your debts on a piece of paper and threw it into the fire as a symbol of being debt free. For most of us it was quite an emotional experience.

"Then Hank closed out the evening by sharing the Harvest Principle. Remember what the Harvest Principle stated? It says 'The seed is the future. Take care of the seed and the seed will take care of you'."

Carolyn paused for a moment and slowly turned, looking out into the darkness. As if on cue, the sun broke through the darkness and began to light the horizon.

Still looking outside, Carolyn continued. "Your future begins now. It's a new day. And this day is filled with opportunity but only for those who take advantage of it."

Roger cleared his throat and took a sip of coffee from a large coffee mug with the words "The Law Of The Seed" stenciled on one side of it.

"We wanted to share with you one of our favorite spots to watch the sunrise." He walked over to Carolyn and put his arm around her waist. "No matter how many times we have been up here, we have never tired of watching the sun rise. For us it represents a new beginning. Yesterday is gone…today has begun."

"Well folks," continued Roger as he turned around facing the group. "Today is a new day, a very exciting day. We have so much that we are going to share with you. This whole day is packed full of training. Are you ready to get started?"

The group's response was weak. Only a few replied.

Roger asked the question again with a little more enthusiasm. "Are you ready to get started?"

This time the group's response was an overwhelming "Yes!"

"Alright then, let's begin."

Roger and Carolyn rolled two large white boards in front of the loft opening blocking the rise of the sun.

Roger started. "All farmers have something in common. Does anyone know what that is?"

The room was silent. Then Maurice, a good natured, quick wit, and class clown raised his hand.

"Go ahead Maurice."

"Well, one thing that they have in common is that half of their clothes come from feed and seed dealers."

The group laughed.

"That was pretty good Maurice, but that is not exactly the answer I was looking for, but now that you mention it, you may be right."

"Besides wearing clothes from the feed and seed suppliers, all farmers have this in common, they know the 'Law of the Seed'. And the ones that fully understand and apply the 'Law of the Seed' are successful. These are the ones that always have a bountiful harvest."

"Listen to me carefully." Roger lowered his voice forcing the group to strain to hear his next statement. "The Law of the Seed is not just for farmers. It's for everyone. It's for you. Know it, understand it, and apply it and you will be successful also."

Moving to the whiteboard on the right side of the group, Roger began to write.

The Garden Plan

THE HARVEST PRINCIPLE
The seed is the future.
Take care of the seed and
the seed will take care of you.

Then directly beneath the statement he wrote in large bold letters.

= HARVEST

Moving to the opposite whiteboard Roger drew five lines with the "plus" symbol at the end of each line.

```
_____ +
_____ +
_____ +
_____ +
_____ +
```

Then in front of the lines he wrote "The Law of the Seed."

The	_____	+
Law	_____	+
Of	_____	+
The	_____	+
Seed	_____	+

"The Law of the Seed is a formula. It is a system made up of five key rules." The first rule is 'Plan.'"

| The | **PLAN** | + |
| Law | _____ | + |

42

The Law Of The Seed

Of	_____	+
The	_____	+
Seed	_____	+

"Successful farmers do not just go out, plow the fields and plant. They plan. They plan for the harvest by planning for the individual seed. Every aspect of farming is about accomplishing the plan."

"Today we are going to plan for the harvest by planning for the seed just like a farmer does."

"Carolyn is going to hand out some bags of seed to you now. Whether you are here as a couple, or by yourself, just take one bag please."

Carolyn walked through each of the rows of bales handing out the bags of seed. Jim and Jenny were handed a bag labeled "Unknown Seed."

Jenny held the bag of seed in her hands. She estimated that it weighed around five pounds. On the front of the bag was a large white label that had "Seed Type, Type of Soil and Planting Instructions," printed along the side.

Seeing that his wife was handing out the last seed bag, Roger continued his talk. "My lovely assistant has just handed out enough seed to plant one full acre of vegetables which is enough to feed all of us many times."

"Each of you is holding a type of seed that is unique. Some of you have carrot seed, others corn, lettuce, radishes, cucumbers, peas, beans and onions. The seeds are unique because for one thing, that seed will only produce one type of vegetable and the second thing is that it requires its own special planting instructions."

"Today we are going to plant those seeds but before we can, we must plan for them."

The Garden Plan

Roger motioned for his wife to continue as he reached for his coffee cup.

Carolyn walked over to Maurice, took his bag and held it up for the group to see. "Maurice and Joy have a bag of corn seed. On the label it says, 'Plant in blocks of 2-3 rows; Rows 24" to 36" apart; Space Seed 12-18" apart; Plant Seed in ½-1" depth. Corn grows tall.'"

Carolyn walked over to another couple. "On this bag it says, 'Cucumber seed. Plant in rows 5ft apart; Space Seed 12-14" apart; Plant Seed in ½-1" depth. Needs lots of sun.'"

"Now it's time for you all to plan your garden. You must all work together to plan your garden. Roger and I have set up a large map in the center of the room which outlines the one acre area that is yours. We have also set some pencils out for you so that you can mark up the map."

"Alright, I think that is about it." Turning to Roger, "Roger did I miss anything?"

"You may want to ask if there are any questions."

"You're right, Honey. Does anyone have any questions before we get started with planning our garden?"

Jenny raised her hand.

"Yes Jenny."

"Carolyn, Jim and I have a bag that says 'Unknown Seed'. And the planting instructions are all blank. How are we supposed to plan for this?"

"Oh yes, I almost forgot about those seeds. Well, all I can say is, plan for the unexpected."

"Carolyn, I'm not sure if I understand?"

"I'm sorry Jenny that's all I can say."

Turning away from Jenny, Carolyn addressed the rest of the group. "Alright, if there are no more questions we will let you go and plan away. You all have about 45 minutes to plan before breakfast."

The Law Of The Seed

Jenny sat there as the rest of group got up and moved to the center of the room to work on the garden plan.

"Jim?"

Jim was already standing. Turning around he saw that Jenny was still sitting and staring at the bag of seed. "Jenny what is it?"

"I just don't get it. Why would they give us this? We don't know what kind of seed this is and we don't even know how to plant it. How are we supposed to plan for this seed?"

"Jenny, maybe we are not supposed to plan for it?"

A little startled by his answer, Jenny looked into Jim's face to figure out what he meant.

"You see I figure we don't plant this seed at all. We don't know what it is. For all we know it could be weed seed."

"Weed seed?"

"Or it could even be real vegetables. But we don't know. And as farmers why would we plant something that we know nothing about; we wouldn't."

A look of relief spread across Jenny's face. "Your right Jim; we wouldn't."

Jenny looked at the bag of seed again, turning it over in her hands. "You know Jim, Roger and Carolyn are pretty tricky."

"Come on Jenny, let's join the rest of the group."

Jim and Jenny made their way to the group. Everyone was circled around a large piece of paper that was taped down unto four folding tables.

The paper had grid lines on it. Over the grid lines someone had outlined, what appeared to be tracts of land. Some of the tracts were identified with labels; "Garden 1,

The Garden Plan

Garden 2". There was one outlined in red that read, "New Garden–1 Acre".

There was a lot of discussion but no one had made any marks on the map yet.

Jim interrupted the group's discussion, "Has anyone ever planted a garden before?"

"I have," came a man's voice from across the table. It was the young muscular man.

The man walked over to Jim. "Growing up on a small family farm we planted many gardens."

"That's great. Could you help organize us and show us how you would plant the garden?" Jim asked.

"Sure. The first thing we did was plant the corn on one end of the garden so that it wouldn't shade the smaller plants."

Maurice piped in. "We have the corn seed. I'll go ahead and pencil in the corn here." Maurice pointed to a small section on the plan.

"Next, we would plant green beans and peas."

A lady's voice came from behind Jenny, "I have the bean seed."

Pretty soon everyone's seed was accounted for and mapped out on the garden plan.

It was Maurice that noticed that Jim and Jenny's seed was not written down on the garden plan. "Hey, Jim and Jenny where is your seed?"

"We're not sure what kind of seed we have so we decided not to plant them," replied Jenny.

"Well, that seems like a waste. Let me look at the seed, maybe Farmer Stud can figure it out," Maurice said with a little chuckle as he took the bag of seed from Jenny.

"Hey Big Guy, can you tell us what kind of seed this is?" Maurice asked.

The Law Of The Seed

Opening up the package he poured some of the seed in his hand. "I'm not quite sure. It looks like carrot but…"

Maurice grabbed the bag, "Carrot seed. Perfect, we have a spot right here that we could plant the seed." Maurice placed the bag on the map and began to write in "carrot seed" on the garden plan.

Jim moved next to Maurice and placed his hand on Maurice's shoulder and leaned over and took the seed off of the map. "Maurice, thanks for trying to help but we are not going to plant our seed. We're not 100% sure what kind of seed it is… it could be weed seeds."

Just then the Gathering Bell rang.

"Perfect timing," Jenny said. "All this planning has made me hungry."

Roger and Carolyn, who had been observing from across the room, walked up to the group. "You guys did a good job. I must say that I think you did the best job so far of any of the groups that we have had in here. Everything looks well thought out and planned. It looks like it's going to be a great vegetable garden," Roger commented.

"I agree with Roger. You guys worked well together. Well it's time for breakfast. Go on and head downstairs. We'll catch up with you all later."

7
The Preparation

The key is not the will to win... everybody has that. It is the will to prepare to win that is important.
Bobby Knight
1940 – Present, American Coach

The future belongs to those who prepare for it.
Ralph Waldo Emerson
1803-1882, American Poet

Jim and Jenny headed down the stairs with the rest of the group. The fresh smell of coffee, muffins and eggs greeted everyone as they made their way to their table. Each table had plates and bowls filled with scrambled eggs, bacon, blueberry muffins, toast, and pitchers of orange juice, hot cocoa and coffee. The center of the table was decorated with a large fresh-cut vase of flowers. From within the vase rising above the bouquet was a sign that read, *"Thought for the Morning – Do not love sleep or you will grow poor. Stay awake and you will have food to spare. Proverbs 14:23"*

Jenny saw the sign and had to laugh to herself. *Funny. Funny.* She thought. Just as she sat down Jim saw the same sign and poked her in the ribs. Jenny caught his little grin, which was followed by a quick wink.

Soon the tables were filled. Everyone was talking about what Roger and Carolyn had said and the Imagine Circle from the night before. They were guessing at what was in store for them today when Hank appeared dressed in

The Law Of The Seed

coveralls and wearing a white apron with the words "Love Your Cook" stitched across the front.

"Good morning everyone." Stopping halfway between the rows of tables he continued, "It's a beautiful day and I'm really glad that you have decided to wake up, get dressed and join us for breakfast. Let's start the day with a word of prayer and then we can eat." With that Hank prayed and then disappeared into the kitchen.

The food was good. Everyone was nearly finished with their breakfast when Ray made his way up on stage to the microphone.

"Boy, wasn't that some good home cookin'? I love eating here. Cindy also likes eating here because she doesn't have to cook at home."

"Well enough about the food, we need to begin our next session. You all ready?"

Before anyone could respond Ray grabbed the mic from the stand and walked over to the whiteboard while he was talking. "Alright, this morning Roger and Carolyn shared with you the first principle of The Law of the Seed. Well, I am going to share the next principle."

Ray pushed the whiteboard to the front and then walked down from the stage to the floor.

"This morning I poked my head in as you guys were planning your garden and I overheard that one of you had some farming experience…now…who…was that?"

Maurice started pointing to the table next to them. "It's the big guy over there, Ray."

Ray walked over to the table. "Is it you?"

"Yah."

"So what is your name?"

"My name is Dan."

"So Dan tell me about your farming experience."

The Preparation

"It's really nothing. I grew up on a small 36 acre farm in Oregon with my two brothers and sister. My parents planted a garden each year and we all helped."

"Was it fun?"

"I'm not sure I would say it was fun. I was forced to help. I had to get up early each morning to do my chores, which included pulling weeds in the garden…"

Ray interrupted Dan. "Come on, you had to have some fun. Didn't you drive the tractor or have garden fights with your brothers?"

"Now that you mention it, I did enjoy driving the tractor and having blueberry fights with my brothers."

"Cool. Blueberry fights. I'm sure your mom loved washing those clothes?"

"Ya, she did get pretty upset with us."

"Alright Dan, I have some serious questions for you. You ready?"

"Sure."

"Okay. Now Dan you can only answer these questions with one word answers. The first question is, after your parents planned out the garden and before you kids planted the seed, what did you do?"

"Can I use two words to answer that?"

"Sorry Dan. Only one word."

"Spread."

"Dan, that's your word? Spread?"

"Well, I wanted to say 'spread manure' but you said one word."

"Alright, I will let you use two words because I am a nice guy."

"Now Dan, why did you guys spread out the manure?"

"To fertilize the soil."

The Law Of The Seed

"Good. Now after you fertilized the soil what did you guys do next?"

"Plow."

"One word answer. I'm proud of you Dan. So after you guys fertilized, you then plowed up the field. And then what?"

"Disk."

"Another one word answer. Dan you are getting the hang of this." Ray turned and looked around the room. "For those of you who do not know what disk is, let me explain. Disking the field is not throwing old computer discs onto the field. Instead it is an attachment that fits on the back of a tractor that cuts the soil up. In fact, you are going to have a chance to participate in disking the fields today. So you will see firsthand how this is done."

"Alright Dan, after you applied fertilizer, plowed and disked the field what did you do next?"

"Raked."

"Dan, you definitely have got the one word thing down."

"Why did you rake?"

"Well my dad would hook up a rake attachment to the tractor and rake the field to rake up any leftover plant material and to level the ground. After that we would use hand rakes to grab the smaller debris and rocks."

"Dan, here is the million dollar question? You ready?"

"Bring it on."

"Spreading manure, plowing, disking, and raking… can you sum up these activities for us with one word?"

Just then the theme from Jeopardy was played over the speakers. Everyone laughed.

"What is, prepare?"

"That's it! Dan, that is exactly the word I was looking for."

The Preparation

Ray patted Dan on the back. "Good job Dan."

The group gave Dan a round of applause.

Ray jogged up the stairs and went straight to the whiteboard and wrote:

The	**PLAN**	+
Law	**PREPARE**	+
Of	_____	+
The	_____	+
Seed	_____	+

"Alright farmers, there it is, the first two principles. Before you can plant any seeds you have to have a plan. And then you must prepare the soil. Everyone with me?"

Ray scanned over the various tables, everyone was nodding their heads. Suddenly the silence was interrupted by the loud sound of a tractor pulling up in front of the barn.

"That folks, is the sound of your farm chariot," Ray said with a smile. "Well, in a few minutes you and I are going to take a little trip to your garden spot. When we get there we will begin preparing the soil for the seed."

Ray glanced at his watch and then looked up at the group. "We have a tight schedule today so let's take a quick 13 minute break. So please go quickly to your room, grab whatever you need for the day and I'll see you at the farm chariot. See you in 13 minutes."

Jim and Jenny returned to their room. Jenny packed a small backpack with a camera, some work gloves, a few water bottles, their straw hats and a few other essentials. Returning to the barn they climbed aboard their farm chariot which ended up being two trailers attached to the unmistakable green tractor, a large John Deere. The trailers were covered and each had six rows of benches that could

The Law Of The Seed

comfortably hold four adults. Behind the last row of benches was a narrow platform, a place for a tour guide.

"It looks like everyone is on board," crackled Ray's voice over the intercom. "If everyone could turn around and look to the back of the chariots, I would like to introduce you to a couple of people."

For Jim and Jenny they had no need to turn around, they had taken a seat at the very back of the trailers right next to Ray and Cindy. It was Jenny's idea to sit in the very back and what a great spot it was.

"Alright, first I want to point out that my boss is joining us. Actually, this is my wife, Cindy. She is the one that keeps me in line and focused on the job at hand. She will be helping us this morning, as we prepare the land for planting."

"Next, I want to introduce you to two great kids. They are Hank and Sue's children, Heather and Caleb. Heather is 13 and she will be our official tour guide this weekend, Caleb is 11 and he will be the chariot driver this weekend. Can everyone say 'hi' to Heather and Caleb?"

The group said 'hi' in unison.

"Hi to you too and welcome aboard everyone," Heather cheerfully responded. "Before we drop you off at your garden, Caleb and I are going to take you on a short 20 minute tour of Ripple Farms. Sound good to you all?"

The group whistled and applauded in agreement.

"Great. Let me put on some driving music and we will be off. Caleb, are you ready?"

Caleb responded with two quick blasts of the large air horns.

"Here comes the music and here we go." The theme song from Chariots of Fire came over the speaker. Jim and Jenny laughed, as did the rest of the group.

The Preparation

As soon as the music started the engine roared to life and jerked forward a few feet, stopped, went another few and then stopped again.

"Quit playing Caleb," came Heather's voice over the speakers.

"New song please." It was Caleb's voice now.

"Alright. Alright."

Heather played the next tune. It was the theme from Bonanza, an old western classic.

Now more of the group began to laugh.

Caleb's voice came through the speaker. "We are just havin' some fun. Dad says laughing is good for the soul."

Next came the sound of the tune, 'Charge'.

Caleb revved the engine and with a gentle start, the group was off.

"Here we go."

Jim and Jenny were amazed by the 20 minute tour. The tour wound through the 550 acre farm. There were horses, cows, and hundreds of acres of crops. There were rows of corn, beans, potatoes, lettuce, onions, carrots and radishes. There were also areas of what appeared to be fresh plantings and some areas where the plants were already peeking through the soil.

It was after a small bend in the road that Jenny saw a large wooden pole barn off in the distance. "Jim, I bet that is where we are going to stop."

"I think you are right Jen."

Sure enough as soon as the tractor came within 50 yards, Caleb began to throttle back. Soon they came to rest just at the front of the pole barn. Under the large canopy were a number of picnic tables.

"Alright everyone, we're here," crackled Heather's voice over the intercom. "Welcome to Lookout Station and...if

The Law Of The Seed

you look out the left side of the trailer you will see why we call it Lookout Station."

A steady sound of awe arose as the group began looking. Jim and Jenny looked left also. The view was breathtaking. The 20 minute ride had ended up on top of a small hill which overlooked the entire farm. In the distance the barn and stables were barely visible due to a light fog that lay around the bottom.

Heather gave the group time to soak in the beauty of the farm before continuing with the rest of the instructions. "Well folks, this is where you get off. Thank you for choosing Ripple Farms' Chariot Service to fulfill your transportation needs."

The group exited the trailers and made their way under the pole barn. The pole barn was quite large. Along one side and one end of the barn were large concrete walls that were divided into four sections with each section containing rich dark soil and the other bins, with various fertilizers. Just in front of the large concrete bins were two well worn wooden tables. In the center of the barn were a half a dozen picnic tables.

"Everyone gather 'round," Ray instructed the group. "Well, it's time for us to get our garden ready. If you brought anything with you just leave it on the picnic tables we'll be back later. Everyone follow me, our garden is just across the drive."

Ray led the group across the road through a line of oak trees into a grassy clearing. "This is it. This is going to be where you plant your garden. As you can see we have the area marked with bright colored stakes."

"Now can anyone, besides Dan, tell me the first thing we do in preparing for the seed?"

"Throw manure!" someone shouted.

The Preparation

"That answer can only come from Maurice." Ray looked around to find him. Spotting him standing in the back of the group, Ray asked, "Maurice, why do we spread manure?"

"To make the ground smell bad."

"Try again."

"To fertilize the ground."

"Maurice is right. Many soils need fertilizer. A lot of times we will use fertilizer nutrient mixers like, 5-10-10 or even 6-6-6. If the soil is too acidic we may use lime and if the soil is alkaline we can acidify it by adding iron sulfate or aluminum sulfate." Ray paused for a moment.

"Listen carefully everyone. I need you to hear and understand my next statement." Ray crouched down on one knee. "We reap what we sow." Ray bent over and scooped up some dirt.

"For the seed to flourish and yield a bountiful harvest, you need to build up the soil and add nutrients. If you do not build up the soil, well…let's say, you get what you deserve."

"Farming takes time. It takes careful planning and diligent preparation." Standing back up, Ray looked around. "Does everyone understand what I just said? Everyone was nodding. "Good."

"With that said, I need a volunteer. I need someone who can multi-task, listen to instruction, is not easily distracted, who is not fearful of a challenge, and who is super-human, which means it has to be a woman. Do I have a volunteer?"

Jim grabbed Jenny's arm and raised it. Jim did it so quickly that Jenny didn't even have time to resist.

"Why Jenny Smith, thank you so much for volunteering. Jenny, if you don't mind please go back to Lookout Station and see my wife, Cindy. She has something to show you."

Jenny gave Jim 'the look' and then disappeared through the trees.

The Law Of The Seed

"And for the rest of you, we have some work to do before she returns. We have some fertilizer mix that needs to be spread. Lady Farmers please grab a guy and have them push the wheelbarrows around while you spread the fertilizer mix around with the shovels."

Just over an hour passed and the spreading of fertilizer was almost complete when Jenny appeared driving a John Deere tractor. She drove straight into the center of the garden and began to plow. There were three plows attached to the tractor. The soil gently rolled over as the plows dug through the layer of grass.

As Jenny made her first turn, she plowed past the group who were clapping and whistling. Jenny paid no attention, she was totally focused on her task. Jim was shocked to see Jenny operating the tractor. She rarely ran the riding lawnmower at home. Watching her run the tractor, it appeared as if she had been doing it all her life.

It didn't take Jenny long to plow the acre tract of land. She raised the plows and pulled up in front of Ray and shut down the engine.

"Well done Jenny. You looked like a true farmer. Farmers, what do you think?"

Again the cheers, whistles and clapping erupted. Jenny rose from her seat with a big smile and gave a bow to the group. She was definitely enjoying the moment.

Ray looked over at his wife, "Cindy, would you take Joy and show her how to disk?"

Joy did not hesitate at all. She walked right up to Cindy. "I'm ready."

Jenny gave Joy a "high-five" as they passed. Cindy and Joy climbed up on the tractor together. Cindy stood directly behind Joy and began to provide her instructions. Soon the tractor was started and they were off.

The Preparation

"I hope you guys have insurance," Maurice joked. "Joy almost ran me over twice at home with our lawnmower."

"Are you sure it wasn't on purpose?" Ray playfully responded.

Joy returned with Cindy still by her side. They had switched attachments and were cutting up the freshly plowed ground with large metal disks. Cindy had Joy make several passes across the garden. The ground began to take shape. Soon Joy was complete and Cindy was instructing another Lady Farmer how to operate the tractor with the rake attachment. The new operator drove around the entire garden, leveling the ground and raking up the leftover plant material.

"You guys did a terrific job. We are now ready to plant seed which we will do right after lunch. Cindy and I will be leaving you now. We have some things that we have to do to prepare for tonight. Joe and Linda will be taking our place and they will be sharing with you the next principle of the Law of the Seed. So head back to Lookout Station where lunch is waiting for you."

The farmers headed back to Lookout Station. The physical work and the heat were wearing out the team. Lunch was exactly what they needed to get refreshed.

8
Taking Action

Knowing is not enough; we must apply.
Willing is not enough; we must do.
Johann Wolfgang Von Goethe
1749-1832, German Poet, Dramatist, Novelist

Be great in act, as you have been in thought.
William Shakespeare
1564-1616, British Poet, Playwright, Actor

Ice cold sweet tea, water, and sodas awaited the group, including sandwiches, watermelon, bags of chips and fresh-baked cookies. It didn't take long for the group to fill their plates and begin eating.

Jim and Jenny were running a little behind the rest of the group. Jenny wanted Jim to take a picture of her on the tractor. Jenny was particularly proud in accomplishing something new. Jim was also very proud of her and he let her know it. Jim also began to see a change in Jenny. She really was enjoying the farm life. It was good to see her so happy and proud of her accomplishment.

Jim and Jenny filled their plates and decided to sit next to one of the single women in the group. She was the last operator on the tractor. Her name was Sharon, a recent divorcee with three kids. Having no one to share her experience with, Jim and Jenny wanted to let her know how impressed they were.

"Sharon, you did a great job on the tractor," commented Jenny. "You picked it up quicker than I did."

Sharon was still beaming from the experience. "Oh, come on. You had the hard part, plowing. I just had to rake."

"No, I mean you just jumped on it and with a quick instruction from Cindy, you were driving around. It took me a couple of tries just to start it."

Sharon turned to Jenny, "My kids are never going to believe it."

"Same with mine."

"For a small fee from both of you, I will let the kids know what you two did," Jim interjected.

Jenny and Sharon both playfully punched him in the arm.

"If I could have everyone's attention…? I'm Joe Redden and this is my wife, Linda. We are going to begin in about five minutes. So if you can finish up your lunch, that will be great."

Jim was just finishing up his sandwich, but Jenny still had not taken even a bite out of hers.

"I guess I better stop talking and start eating."

With his mouth full, Jim just nodded in agreement.

It was more like ten minutes before Joe got up to speak. "I apologize for the delay, but we are waiting for the farm chariot. Caleb said they had to make a quick pit stop. But I guess the quick pit stop is not so quick! It should only be a couple more minutes."

"I wonder where we are going?" asked Jenny. "It seems kind of strange since our garden is here, and I thought we were going to plant the seeds next."

"Yah it does Jen, but that's alright because it gives me a chance to get some more of those delicious cookies." With that Jim was off.

The unmistakable horn sounded off in the distance. "Alright everyone, it sounds like our chariot is almost here.

The Law Of The Seed

Go ahead and grab some drinks if you like. And don't worry about getting your things, we'll return later for them," instructed Joe.

Heather's voice came over the intercom. "We're sorry that you had to wait. Caleb and I had to drop off our business plan and it took a little longer than we thought."

Jim, who had just taken a seat in front of Heather, turned around and asked, "business plan—for what?"

Acknowledging Jim, Heather repeated the question into the intercom, "Mr. Jim wants to know what the business plan is for. Caleb, can you answer the question?"

"Of course," came Caleb's enthusiastic voice over the speakers. "This coming summer there is a group of us that are planting, what dad says, 'an entrepreneur seed'. We are starting a business to make some money. And the first step, according to the Law of the Seed, is 'plan'. So we wrote up a business plan for our parents to review."

"And approve," interjected Heather.

"Hopefully, they will like it, because we are really excited and want to start working on step number two, preparing for the business."

"Well, enough about that, we have got to get going," Heather said changing subjects. "As a safety reminder, please keep all arms, legs and heads inside the farm chariot." Before Heather released the talk button, she was overheard telling Jim, "I've always wanted to do that."

The theme song from Gilligan's Island came over the speakers and then they were off.

The ride took them off of the main gravel road and through the fields, finally ending in an area of half grown vegetables. "This is your stop. You may disembark now," Heather instructed the group in a very professional tone.

Taking Action

"Come on over here," Joe directed the group. "Linda and I wanted to show you a garden planted about a month ago. Tell me, what do you see?"

Jim and Jenny looked over the garden. They really didn't know what they were looking at but there were plants everywhere. And nothing seemed to be planted in rows, like their team had planned to do with their garden.

Linda broke the silence. "Let me help you. Look over the garden and tell me if you see any bare spots?"

Several group members pointed to an area that looked like there should have been vegetables planted.

"Good. Now this bare spot probably did have some seeds but they were probably planted too deep or the seeds were overwatered and they rotted. Can someone point out any plants that look weak or the leaves have a light green color to them?"

Jim walked a little deeper into the garden, "what about these plants here?" Jim pointed to a whole section of plants.

Joe and Linda walked over. "Perfect. Everyone come over here. Look at these vegetables. Notice how weak they look. And look at the shade of green of the leaves. This is a result of not having enough sunlight. This group planted this vegetable too close to the corn and the oak trees, both of which would provide lots of shade."

"Last one, can someone point out a vegetable plant whose leaves are yellow and kind of sickly looking?"

"Right here," responded Dan.

Linda looked over at Dan, who was crouched down. "Perfect example. Can you tell me why they are yellowish in color?"

Dan looked down at his feet, "Since my feet are getting wet, I say because of too much water."

The Law Of The Seed

"You're right, they are getting too much water due to poor drainage. You can see how the water is just collecting there. The ground was not properly leveled before they planted."

Linda stood up and wiped her hands on her jeans. "Well, we are done here. Let's all get back on the farm chariot, and we will continue our discussion as soon as we get back to our garden."

The group boarded the chariot and soon were back at their garden. Joe motioned for everyone to sit on a section of the grass which was slightly sloped and just above their garden.

Joe and Linda rolled a couple of wheelbarrows in front of the group. Then Joe propped a large poster board against the pair of wheelbarrows. The poster board had the planting plan taped to it.

Joe spoke first. "So far today you have learned that every successful farmer plans first. They plan for the seed. The second thing is that they prepare for the seed, which by looking at the freshly prepared soil behind me, you have done a good job. The next principle is to take action, to plant."

"You plan, you prepare, you plant." That is the sequence to becoming a successful farmer."

"Now planting is not as easy as you may think. You saw firsthand, how one of the groups planted the seeds incorrectly. The result being that the garden will produce little to no harvest at all."

"Linda and I were looking over your plan and we are quite impressed. You all did a good job on paper, organizing the various vegetables, according to their..."

"Do you have suggestions for us to improve our layout before we start?" Someone yelled out, interrupting Joe.

Joe's expression changed instantly. "Whoever asked that please come up here now."

The group became silent. Everyone began looking around nervously, not sure what to expect. No one moved. After a few seconds, which seemed like a couple of minutes, Dan stepped forward, with his wife in tow, holding his hand. "I asked the question," Dan stammered.

"Why?"

"Because…because nothing is ever perfect and I thought that…well, I thought that you both could help us by offering some suggestions. I didn't want our garden to end up like the garden we visited."

"Is that the real reason?"

Dan lowered his head and stared at the ground.

Jim was surprised by Dan's behavior. Dan was a big muscular guy who appeared to be a natural leader, who never was intimidated.

"I didn't want to let the team down."

"Let the team down?" Joe asked.

"Yah, the layout that you were looking at was based on my childhood experience with gardening. I just didn't want the garden to fail, like…."

Joe's serious expression turned into a warm smile. "Dan, for a big guy you are quite humble, *and* you are also pretty smart. I wish every group that has come through here had someone like you."

Dan looked puzzled. Jim too was stumped by Joe's response.

Linda whispered something in Joe's ear. Joe shook his head slowly and then turned his attention to the group. He looked around and saw that his response to Dan had caused some anxiousness among the team. "I'm sorry everyone for being so intense. I was totally caught off guard by Dan's question. You see, of the groups that we have led, no one yet has asked for our help—which I find odd. Linda and I are here to help."

"A wise man named Solomon once wrote that 'Plans fail for lack of counsel, but with many advisors they succeed.' We are your advisors and Dan recognized that. The others did not recognize that and you can see how their plans are turning out." Turning to Dan, Joe held out his hand, "You, my man, deserve a big atta boy."

"Linda, would you answer Dan's question?

"Love to," responded Linda enthusiastically. "But rather than give you an answer outright, let's see if we can discover it together."

Linda grabbed the poster board and started walking into the center of the field. "Come on everyone, please circle around the plan...and make sure that you can see it."

Linda laid the poster board with the plan taped to it right on top of the ground. She spun the board around to orient the North symbol on the plan to actual North.

"From what we have learned looking at the other garden, take a look at the plan that you all came up with and then look at your physical space now. Do you see a potential problem?"

Jenny saw it immediately. "I see a problem."

"Go ahead and tell us."

"Well, this area has a lot of shade." Jenny pointed to one corner on the plan. Turning around and pointing to the trees, "You can see that the trees are providing a lot of shade. I think we should move these vegetables over to the other end. Where there is more sun."

"Jenny, that is very observant. In fact, that is one of the two things that Joe and I found wrong with this plan. Good job. Can someone point out the second problem?"

Taking Action

No one could. "I know it's a tough one to identify but we noticed that the ground right here," Linda pointed to a spot on the plan, "This is not flat but rather bowl shaped. It will not properly drain and the seeds will rot due to standing water."

"Stand back and crouch down. You will see what I mean."

Jim got down on all fours and looked into the direction of the bowl area. *Unbelievable. I would have never seen that,* he thought.

"Man, I would have never seen that," Maurice belted out. "So what should we do?"

"It really is a simple fix. All we need to do is to take the rake and level off the area a little better."

A couple of guys grabbed some rakes and began to move some dirt around to level off the area. It didn't take long. One by one the team crouched down on all fours and saw that the area was level.

"I think you are ready to plant. Let's get started."

Joe continued, "We are going to divide you into two groups, one group will go with Linda and plant part of the garden and the other group will go with me."

Joe divided the group according to the vegetable seed. The planting began.

It was hard work. Linda assigned Jim and Jenny to make sure that the seeds were planted according to what was written on the seed bags, since they did not have any seeds to plant. Primarily to make sure that the seeds were spaced properly apart and that they were planted and covered to the proper depth.

There were a couple of times that Joe could be heard yelling "Sow sparingly, reap little! Sow generously, reap much!"

The Law Of The Seed

Hours passed. The team of farmers were finally done. Everyone was exhausted. Not used to physical work and working during the heat of the day had worn everyone out.

Joe instructed everyone to take a seat on the ground. Many just collapsed and lay on the ground.

"Both Linda and I want to tell you all that it was an honor to work alongside of you. You all worked well together and you worked hard. If I was a betting man, I would say that this garden here will probably have the best harvest of any garden that we have planted to date. You guys were careful on how you planted the seed. You spaced them correctly and you planted each type of seed to the proper depth. A lot of care was taken. A job well done."

"If you guys don't mind we would like to take a group photo, and then we have something special that we would like to share with you."

Some of the lady farmers expressed their disapproval of the photos because of the way they looked. But in the end it didn't matter. Joe and Linda still took the photos.

"Well, we would like to reward you all with something special... a Ripple Farms old fashioned shower. Let 'er rip kids!"

Just then the area was flooded with water coming from all directions. Heather, Caleb, Chase and Hunter had quietly hooked up hoses to the high pressure irrigation lines while everyone was diligently working. Taking cover behind the tractor and the trees, they were well hidden from the exhausted team of farmers.

First, there were screams from some of the group members and some tried to run, but there was no escape. Soon everyone was just laughing and enjoying the moment.

Jenny tried to run away as soon as the first drops of water fell, but Jim tripped her up and she fell to the ground. Jim grabbed one of her legs and rolled her over. Jim then fell to the ground next to her and closed his eyes as the refreshing cool water showered them both. *Now this is fun.*, he thought.

The Law Of The Seed

9
Putting The Pieces Together

Coming together is a beginning.
Keeping together is progress.
Working together is success.
Henry Ford
1863-1947, American Founder of the Ford Motor Company

Jim and Jenny returned to their room, wet and exhausted. As Jim unlocked the room door and pushed it open for Jenny, she saw an envelope on the floor, along with two pieces of thin plywood that appeared to be part of a large jigsaw puzzle.

Jenny picked up the two pieces of the plywood and laid them on the coffee table and then opened the envelope to find a card inside. On the front of the card was a picture of the red barn with "Ripple Farms" written underneath it. Inside was a note from the Ripple Team. Jenny read it to Jim.

"Greetings Financial Farmers,

We know that you are tired. So relax...take a nap, sit on the rocker, take a glide on one of the porch swings...just relax. Dinner will not be served until 7:30 p.m. so you have plenty of time to unwind.

Putting The Pieces Together

Tonight we will start putting the pieces together and show you how the activities of today can be applied to your life and to your finances. That is why we want you rested.
See you at 7:30 p.m. in the barn.

Ripple Farms' Team

P.S. Please bring your piece of the jigsaw puzzle."

"That's great. I really could use a long nap," Jim responded as he was taking off his dirty clothes. "Jen, if it's okay, I am going to jump in the shower...unless...you want to go first?"

"Go ahead Jim, that's fine."

Jenny picked up one of the jigsaw puzzle pieces and began to look it over. On one side was just plain plywood, however, the other side, was colored light blue and the word "Jim" was written on it. Jenny picked up the other one and it too was light blue in color and her name was written across it. *Very interesting,* she thought.

Jim and Jenny woke up to an announcement coming through the speakers in their room. "Dinner will be served in 30 minutes."

"Wow, did I sleep. I was really tired," yawned Jim.

Jenny rolled over, "I was too. I'm glad that they gave us some time to rest."

Jim and Jenny got dressed, grabbed their two puzzle pieces and headed to the barn for dinner. Just outside their door was Sharon, the single lady who operated the tractor with Jenny.

The Law Of The Seed

"What do guys think this is about?" holding up the puzzle piece in front of them.

"I don't know," responded Jim, "we'll find out soon enough."

The three entered the barn. The dining area was completely transformed. Just inside the double barn doors were three rows of display easels, each showcasing six to eight photos of the days' events. There were photos of the group arriving early in the morning getting coffee, photos of the group watching the sunrise, including photos of Jenny, Joy and Sharon on the tractors, there was even was a picture of Jim laying on the ground, all wet, with his eyes closed, and wearing a huge smile.

The tables were arranged into two semi-circle rows with seating on one side, all facing towards the stage. Each table was covered with a white table cloth, colored by navy blue cloth napkins. The center of the tables had 2-3 potted plants.

Up on stage, a video was playing of the day's events. The video was made up of photos that were taken throughout the day. Music played while the photos appeared. Each photo was accompanied by funny captions.

Directly in front of the stage was something really abnormal. It caught Jenny's attention as soon as she walked through the front doors of the barn. It appeared to Jenny that it was a really large picture frame. There was no picture in it just a large frame. The frame, Jenny estimated to be about six feet tall and at least ten to twelve feet long. The frame was about six inches wide and it had a picture of the farm repeatedly burned into it.

Camp Director Ray's voice sounded, "If everyone would find a seat we can begin. You may sit wherever you like, except for the spots that are marked 'reserved'." Ray waited a few minutes till everyone was seated

Putting The Pieces Together

"Tonight, the Ripple Farms' staff would like to dine with you—so that we can get to know you better. So team come on out and take your seats." The staff came from the kitchen. Hank and Sue, Roger and Carolyn, Joe and Linda, and Cindy, all made their way to various spots around the tables. Roger and Sue ended up sitting next to Jim and Jenny. Ray waited till everyone had taken their seat before saying the blessing.

As soon as Ray had finished praying, the kitchen doors flew open and out came Heather, Caleb, Chase, Hunter and six other kids, carrying plates of food.

"Now this is service," Maurice bellowed, loud enough for the entire group to hear.

The meal consisted of fresh garden salad with onions, radishes and tomatoes; fresh baked bread, mashed potatoes, fresh-picked green beans, and a choice of fried chicken, or pork chops.

Ray jumped back on stage, just as everyone was finishing up. "Didn't the kids do a great job?" he asked. The group responded with cheers, whistles and applause. "As I'm sure you may have guessed, everything we ate here today came from our gardens."

"Before Hank comes up to share with you, we have a little dedication ceremony that we would like to hold first. One of you is going to help me with this dedication…so…if you would carefully pick up your water glass and look underneath for a red sticky dot…"

"It's me Ray, I have the red dot." It was Kari, Big Dan's wife.

"Well, come on up Kari. Folks, as she comes up let me tell you about the dedication and what Kari is going to do. First, Kari is going to represent you all. On behalf of you, she is going to dedicate your garden to two organizations.

The Law Of The Seed

The first organization is a teen crisis pregnancy center. This is a home for young pregnant teenage girls. The girls live there for up to three months. During that time they are taught about caring for their baby and how to cope as a young teen mother."

"The second organization is a group home for kids. This is a home for children that have either run away from home or for kids that the State has taken from their families due to abuse or neglect."

"Six of these kids are here tonight. In fact, we had three from each center serving you. We are going to call these six kids up on stage and have Kari read the dedication. If you are okay with this, say 'yes'."

The group responded with an overwhelming shout of "Yes!"

Looking at his wife, Ray asked, "Honey, would you go ahead and get the kids, and bring them up on stage?"

Cindy rose from her seat and went into the kitchen. Within a few minutes she had all six of the kids up on stage. Ray handed Kari a letter to read.

Kari unfolded the letter and turned toward the six youth. "Today we planted seeds of hope. Today we planted seeds for food. We planned. We prepared. We planted. Today we planted a garden. On behalf of everyone who is seated here, we dedicate our garden of love and with love to New Hope Teen Crisis Pregnancy Center and New Beginnings Group Home. May our garden fill your homes."

The entire group stood to their feet and began to clap. Kari hugged the six kids. One young person in particular was moved and held on to Kari for quite some time.

Ray held up two signs. "Just so you know which garden is yours we are going to place these signs in front of the

Putting The Pieces Together

garden. So when it is time to come and pick your vegetables, you won't pick from someone else's garden."

Ray escorted the kids and Kari off of the stage.

"This is what it's all about…sharing with others," Hank stated as he walked up on stage.

Grabbing a bar stool he moved to the center of the stage and sat down. "Not counting the hard work, or getting up early in the morning, or getting drenched by kids, or the physical demands of being a farmer, is everyone having a good time at Ripple Farms?"

"I sure hope you are. Now tonight, I'm going to make three promises to you. The first is that I guarantee you will have some fun this evening. The second is that you will learn something that you can apply immediately to your financial lives; and third, I promise that to achieve the first two promises, it will not require you to break a sweat. How about that? Well, let's get started."

"Each of you were given a piece of a puzzle…a very large puzzle piece I might add. That piece has your name on it. Believe it or not, you are a key part of the puzzle. Now what I want you to do is to start putting the puzzle together. Take the piece and place it into the picture frame. I will give you one hint. If your piece has a blue color then it goes on top for the sky. If your piece is green … well that goes on the bottom for the ground. Everyone understand?"

"Wait, I have a question," said Jenny. "All the jigsaw puzzles that I worked on were laying flat, not standing straight up like this one. How are we supposed to build this without our pieces falling off?"

"Good question. Jenny, let me answer your question with a question. Do you remember as a kid, using Lincoln Logs to build forts and cabins?"

"That was ages ago."

The Law Of The Seed

"Do you remember?"

"Yes...barely."

"How did you build a fort using the Lincoln Logs?"

"Playing with my brothers we would stack the logs on top of one another."

"How did the logs stay together?"

Jenny's expression changed. She understood. "They stayed together by being snapped together."

"That's it. All of the pieces you have in your hands build upon each other. Just so you know, we also have puzzle pieces that fit along side of yours. So we will be building the puzzle with you."

"Everyone ready? Let's get started."

Jenny looked at Jim as she stood up, "This should be interesting."

The group gathered around the frame. Each of the couples soon realized that their pieces snapped together with each other. It was also discovered that every person had only a frame edge piece. No one had a piece for the interior of the puzzle. Within a few minutes the entire frame along the bottom was complete.

The sides of the puzzle frame took more time. Each person, who had a side edge piece, had to carefully stack their piece by snapping it to the puzzle piece directly underneath theirs. It proved challenging. More than once the pieces collapsed and fell to the floor. But after multiple tries, both sides of the frame were built. All that remained was the frame edge along the top.

Jim and Jenny realized their pieces went along the top. It was Jenny who asked, "How are we supposed to hang our pieces along the top? There is nothing supporting them?"

Putting The Pieces Together

The puzzle building came to a halt. Hank stepped forward. "I would like to share a little history with you which should solve our dilemma."

"In ancient Roman times, numerous bridges were built out of stone. The shape of the bridges was arched in a semi circle. I'm sure you remember seeing these on the history channel or in travel brochures. Anyway, these bridge were constructed of large stone blocks that were wedged against each other to form the arch. Now the main stone, the central stone on top of the arch was called the keystone. The keystone was the most important stone. Without it the bridge would collapse. The keystone would be the last stone wedged into place. It kept the arch together."

"Now I know that we are not building an arch, but the same principle can be applied here. Although Sue and I have already used our puzzle pieces, we have another one that is labeled 'Ripple Farms', this is the keystone. This will be the last piece that will be added and snapped into place."

"Now when the Romans built the arch portion of the bridge, they would build a wooden frame first. This would allow the bridge builders to place the stones into position. Then, when the keystone was placed, the wooden frame was removed."

"Our hands are going to be the wooden frame. Each person who has a jigsaw puzzle piece that goes along the top will snap their piece into position and then hold it up until the keystone puzzle piece is snapped into place."

"Ready top row?"

Both Jim and Jenny were pretty excited to see if this would really work. Jim and Jenny snapped their pieces together and then joined their pieces to the top right of the frame. Someone else snapped their piece to Jim and Jenny's

The Law Of The Seed

and then supported it with their hands. A couple of others were building the left side of the frame, at the same time.

Now it was Hank's turn. He gently snapped the keystone puzzle piece to the pieces on both sides of him. "Very gently, let go of your piece," he whispered.

Everyone held their breath. Jim and Jenny let go of their pieces and stepped back. The puzzle frame held.

The group clapped and gave each other 'high fives'.

"Quite an accomplishment everyone. It usually takes us a couple of tries…and you all did it on the first try. Good teamwork, Farmers."

"Go ahead and head back to your seats," Hank instructed the group of financial farmers. "My better half is going to come up and share what this puzzle represents."

10
Farmer's Truths

A generous man will prosper;
he who refreshes others will himself be refreshed.
Proverbs 11:25

Truth of Giving — When you share and give of yourself
to help others, you will be refreshed and blessed.

"You are looking at, 'The Puzzle of Success'," Sue said affectionately, as she stood next to the large frame. "The puzzle represents one area of our lives, which for this weekend, is the area of finances. The puzzle could just as well represent our faith, our family, our area of fitness, our friendships, our firm, or our area of fun."

Sue reached down and picked up a puzzle piece from the floor. Holding it up she said, "Each puzzle piece represents a truth or a principle. Individually these pieces provide direction; tips for life. But by combining all of the pieces into your life, it produces a successful harvest."

"Over the years, we observed that successful farmers who followed the Law of the Seed, were also guided by another set of principles. We, at Ripple Farms, call them 'Farmer's Truths'. These truths are life skills and lessons that have been passed down from generation to generation. Let me explain using 'The Puzzle of Success'."

"We just built the border of the puzzle. That border represents each of us. The farmer's truth is that for a person to succeed in life within the area of finances, they need to have a support structure, a group of people and resources that can provide them with advice, direction and encouragement."

Truth of Relationships

Sue walked over to the whiteboard and wrote the words "Farmer's Truths" across the top. Underneath she wrote "Truth of Relationships".

"The Farmer's Truth of Relationships says that 'With many advisors your plans will succeed'. This proved so true for Hank and me personally. When we started networking with the right kind of people, we made new friends and formed new relationships. It was within this circle of friends that we asked for advice about our finances. We received lots of advice and we took their advice to heart and acted on it. Because of those right connections and advice, we were able to climb out of the debt pit and turn things around."

Sue looked at the group, trying to read the expressions on their faces to see if they understood. "Are you all with me? Do you understand…?"

Sharon interrupted Sue, "I think I understand. For me as a new single parent with three kids, I have been stressed about money because my husband used to make all of the financial decisions— and I never had to. But now I have to."

Pointing to the puzzle, Sharon asked, "Since my name is up there on one of those pieces, that means that I am connected with all of you. Does that mean I can call you and ask for help?"

"Absolutely," Sue responded. "But not just us at Ripple Farms but every name that is listed up there."

"Please don't take this the wrong way guys," Sharon commented as she looked around. Looking back at Sue she pressed further, "But why would I call and ask for help from the group when they are messed up just like me? I mean really. If they didn't have financial issues, they wouldn't be here."

Sharon's words stung.

"Sharon, everyone has something to give. You just have to listen and not pre-judge." Now it was Sharon who was stung by the words.

"Sharon, did you know that Jim is an Accountant? He could offer you tax advice, which I couldn't. And Joy works at a bank. She could tell you the best type of savings and checking accounts to set up for you and for your kids. I couldn't."

"Sharon, I could go on and on with probably every person in this room. Everyone has something of value that they could offer advice on—good sound advice."

Realizing what she had said and the tone at which it was said, Sharon looked around the room and apologized for her inconsiderate statement.

Sue, seeing the look of remorse on Sharon's face, turned the moment into a positive. "Sharon brings up a good point. Each of you have experiences and hold various jobs that can benefit the rest of the team. You need to share those with each other. I challenge each of you to learn about everyone's occupation and talent before you leave this weekend. Swap phone numbers and emails. Get to know one another."

Turning to Sharon, "Thank you for asking the question and for being honest."

"If no one has any more questions, I am going to turn it back over to Hank." Sue waited a few seconds and then walked back to her seat and sat down.

"Thank you, Dear." Hank responded from the back of the room. Walking to the front, he carried three long and oddly

The Law Of The Seed

shaped puzzle pieces. He placed them down on the edge of the stage.

"Today you were introduced to the Law of the Seed and were taught the first three principles. Can someone name those three for me?"

Maurice's hand shot straight up.

"Maurice. Go ahead and tell us."

Maurice slid his chair back and stood up. "Plan, prepare and plant."

"Very good. Since you're standing why don't you come on up and help me."

"I thought you would never ask!"

Hank handed Maurice the three puzzle pieces. "Maurice, go ahead and place these three pieces within the puzzle. And be careful, I don't want the puzzle to fall."

Maurice walked over to the puzzle and laid the three pieces on the floor. Looking them over carefully and then looking over the puzzle area, he picked up the piece labeled 'Plan' and turned to the group. Holding the piece up with his left hand he flowingly outlined the puzzle piece with his right hand, much like a magician carefully preparing the prop for his next trick. Exaggerating each step, Maurice carefully placed the piece into position. It snapped together in the far left corner, tying the left and bottom borders together. Standing back, Maurice, the pretend Magician, extended both hands towards the newly placed piece as if to say "Ta Dah!" Maurice continued with his routine with the remaining two pieces. Both puzzle pieces snapped right next to one another.

Hank joining in on the act, "Thank you, Maurice the Great. Good job. Mr. Magnificent can go back to his seat now."

Some of the group members started clapping. Maurice slowly bowed and then blew kisses to the group as he took his seat.

Hank shook his head from side to side and chuckled under his breath. Looking at Joy, "I'm sure there is never a dull moment around your house."

"Never," Joy responded. Then turning to Maurice gave him a gentle peck on the lips.

"Well, what Maurice has so eloquently placed within our puzzle is Plan, Prepare and Plant. These three pieces are the first of five foundational principles – the rules that we must follow for financial success. Now on top of the rules are truths by which we as farmers operate. They are our codes of conduct."

Seeing some blank expressions on some of the members, Hank continued, "Don't worry, this will begin to make more sense as we continue to share tonight."

"Now whether you knew it or not, we have been demonstrating farmer's truths with you all day. Sue shared one of them already; The Truth of Relationships. Well, we have more we want to share with you."

Truth of Attitude

Lifting up the plywood cut puzzle piece for everyone to see, "This piece has the word 'Attitude' written on the back of it. Cindy, would you mind explaining this farmer's truth?"

"Sure." Cindy took a quick sip of water and then stood up and walked up to Hank and took the puzzle piece from him.

"This morning your alarm clock woke you up at 5:10. You had a choice, to sleep in or get up and make the most of today. All of you got up and made the most of today. This piece represents you. We call it the 'Truth of Attitude' and it states that those that act with intention will succeed."

Cindy walked up to the whiteboard and wrote 'Truth of Attitude'.

Placing the cap back on the marker, Cindy moved to the front of the tables standing just in front of Jenny. "I want to share another example of this farmer's truth being demonstrated today." Using the marker as a pointer, Cindy pointed at Jenny. "This Lady Famer and that one and that one," pointing at Joy and Sharon, "are perfect examples of applying the 'Truth of Attitude'. These three Lady Farmers, without hesitation, operated a tractor for the very first time today."

Looking down at Jenny, Cindy continued, "You succeeded with today's challenge because you applied the first two truths; the Truth of Attitude and the Truth of Relationships. You acted. You were self-motivated to learn and try something new. And you listened to counsel, which was me. Good job, Jenny." Looking over at Joy and Sharon, "Nice job, Ladies."

Cindy walked back to the whiteboard and placed the marker back on the tray and went back to her seat.

Jenny felt really proud of herself for what she had done today. Jim rubbed Jenny's back, "Good job, Jen."

"Good example, Cindy," Hank said, as he moved to the front. "I also want to point out that the 'thought of the day' at the breakfast table this morning, represented this truth also. Does anyone remember what that was?"

Jim still rubbing Jenny's back, blurted out, "My Jenny does."

Jenny gave the 'I will get you for this look' and answered sheepishly. "Yes, I remember. It said *'Do not love sleep or you will grow poor. Stay awake and you will have food to spare.'* I believe that's right…I just can't remember the scripture reference though."

"No, that's perfect. Good job, Jenny."

"So far we have shared The Truth of Relationships and the Truth of Attitude. There are more truths that we are going to share this evening, but first let me tie what we have learned so far to money and finances."

"You have to have a plan for your money. Plan is the first rule of the Law of the Seed. You know most people spend more time planning their vacation than planning their finances."

"Let me ask you a question, how many of you have a plan on how you are going to spend your money monthly?"

Only two people raised their hands.

"How many of you have a one year, five year and long range plan for your money?"

No one raised their hands.

"Folks to be a successful financial farmer, you must have a plan…and we can help. We have forms and a step-by-step set of instructions contained in your workbook that will guide you through these steps. When you return home, after this weekend, take time to work on your financial plan."

"The second principle you learned from the Law of the Seed was 'Prepare'. Preparation of your financial soil is important. Just as you prepared the soil with fertilizer and then plowed and raked the field—you must do the same at home. Let me give you an example of what I mean."

Walking up to Jim and Jenny, "Do you mind if I use you two as an example?" Hank asked.

Both Jim and Jenny signaled with their heads that it would be alright.

"Let's say that Jim and Jenny on their 5-year financial plan had a goal to pay off all of their debt except for their

The Law Of The Seed

home. To turn that harvest, another word for goal, into reality, they are going to have to do a few things. The harvest is no debt."

"So one of the first things that I would do is to develop a financial farmer cash flow plan. This plan would show my monthly expenses, like house payment, utility expenses, food, insurance and so on. Then I would look to see what I could reduce. In this case, I found that we were eating out too much and that by eating at home more we could save between $75 and $100 a month. That $100 would be applied to the debt payment."

"Everyone following me so far? What we have done is plan and prepare. Now we need to plant. Remember the harvest for Jim and Jenny is to pay off all of their debt. Planting is action. It is placing the plan and preparation into motion. If I was in Jim and Jenny's shoes what I would do now is to have a portion—$25 of my weekly paycheck direct deposited into a separate account called 'debt payment'. Then each month I would write a check from that account and apply it to a specific debt."

"What we have just done is planted a seed, a $100 seed."

Turning to Jim and Jenny, "You two are on your way to becoming debt free. How do you feel?"

"It feels good...." Jim hesitated for a moment, wondering if he should ask the question *Is it really that simple?*

Hank caught the hesitation in Jim's voice. "Go on Jim—I can tell by the look on your face that you are a little skeptical."

Jim shifted in his seat. "Hank, it all sounds good but can it really be that simple? I mean, if it was that simple, why wouldn't everyone be doing this?"

"Good questions Jim." Hank paused for a moment, fixing his eyes on the back wall, deciding whether or not he should answer the question outright or have the group discover the truth on their own. Taking a deep breath and then slowly exhaling he continued, "You are asking the same questions that many in this group are thinking right now. But rather than answer your question, Jim, I'm going to let you and the group discover the answer on your own. And then tomorrow night we will talk about it."

Jim wasn't too surprised by Hank's answer. He understood that sometimes searching for and discovering an answer is more valuable in developing a person than just giving an answer. Jim looked at Hank and gave him a simple blink with his eyes and nod with his head as if to say 'I understand'.

"Well, we have more that we want to cover but before I call Carolyn up, I think it is time for some dessert. Kids?"

Heather led the group of servers out of the kitchen. Each of the kids were carrying a dessert of freshly-picked strawberries topped with whipped cream layered over the shortcake. Accompanying the shortcake was a scoop of vanilla bean ice-cream and hot flavored coffee.

Maurice seeing the shortcake, ice-cream and coffee could not contain his approval, "Now this is what I'm talkin' about. Honey, I'm ready to give up my day job and become a full-time farmer so I can enjoy this type of food every day!"

Dan chimed in also, "I'm with ya, Man. This is livin'."

"While you are eating the no-calorie dessert, Carolyn is going to come up and share another Farmer's Truth with you."

The Law Of The Seed

Truth of Focus

Carolyn slowly walked up to the front followed by Roger who was pushing a small wooden two-shelf cart. On top of the cart were three brown bags with white labels on them. Roger rolled the cart up to Carolyn and then went back to his seat by Jim and Jenny.

With a smile Carolyn looked at Hank and said, "Thank you for having me speak during dessert. Even though the strawberry shortcake looks real good, it's the calories that are no good for me. So thanks for thinking of me." Carolyn gave him a quick wink.

"Well," Carolyn moved a few steps to the right stopping just in front of Dan and Kari. Looking out at the group, she continued, "I'm sure today has certainly been one of those days that you will not soon forget. I know that it was for me. I will tell you why in a moment."

Taking one of the bags from the cart she handed it to Dan. "Dan, it looks like you are almost done with your dessert so would you mind reading the label and telling me what is in the bag?"

Dan put down his spoon and looked at the label. "The label says 'Corn Seed'."

"And this, what does the label say?" Carolyn handed him the second brown bag and removed the corn seed.

"This one says 'Beans'."

"Last one Dan, read this one for the group."

"There is nothing written on this label." Dan turned the bag over looking for any type of markings. "No, there is nothing on this bag that tells me what it is."

"Thank you, Dan for helping, and I'm sorry that I interrupted your dessert."

Carolyn took the seed package that had no name on it and stepped to the center. "Today, Roger and I handed out various types of vegetable seed and told you to plan for your seed which you all did, most efficiently—you all worked well together."

"We also tried to trip you up with this no name seed that we handed to Jim and Jenny." Moving to the left, Carolyn stood just in front of them. "Jim, Jenny… You two did an outstanding job this morning. You made a very wise decision to not include this seed in the garden."

Jim was already finished with his dessert and was sipping on some coffee when Carolyn turned and looked at him. "Jim, can you tell the group why you and Jenny decided not to plan for this seed?"

Jim put down the cup. "It really was pretty simple. We didn't want to plant something that we had no idea what it was. For all we knew it could have contained weed seed– which I doubt. I think it contained some type of vegetable seed that had a very specific planting requirement."

"Actually Jim, it *was* weed seed. Had you guys planted this seed it would have produced a fast growing weed that would have taken over your garden. It would have choked and killed some of the vegetables and for others it would have slowed the growth."

Jenny, still eating ice cream was perplexed by the weed seed. She put down her spoon and raised her hand just barely above her head.

"Yes Jenny."

"If we had planned to plant this seed, would you have stopped us from planting it?" Jenny asked, still troubled about the weed seed.

"No Jenny, we wouldn't have."

The Law Of The Seed

"But why? I don't understand why you would have had us ruin a nice vegetable garden with weeds."

"To teach a lesson. Remember, you reap what you sow. Today, you two and the rest of the team made a good decision not to plant and that leads me to our next Farmer's Truth: Truth of Focus."

Carolyn went up to the board and wrote down the truth. She returned to Jenny. "This truth says that those that focus on the right goal, succeed. What we did to you and Jim was provide a distraction. But you chose to focus on the goal of planting a garden. Not knowing what was in the package, you avoided the distraction and instead planned out the garden based on what you did know."

Carolyn continued, "I love this truth. It really hit home with me a number of years ago when Roger and I were trying to get out of debt. We had all kinds of distractions that kept trying to derail us from reaching our goal. We had the distraction of the get-rich-quick schemes that would come over the TV and through the mail. We had the distraction of emergencies–those unplanned expenses that you didn't think about, like a car breaking down or needing a root canal. The distraction of friends, who were buying nice homes, cars, and the latest techno gadgets. It was hard. But Roger and I kept the right focus, and together we finished the race of becoming debt free."

Turning back to Jenny, "Would you mind helping me place the 'focus' puzzle piece into the puzzle?"

Carolyn reached underneath the cart and pulled out the wooden puzzle piece and handed it to Jenny. Together they went up to the puzzle and snapped the piece into the proper location.

"We have one more truth that we want to share with you this evening," Hank stated as he rose from his seat. He pushed his chair up to the table and rested both hands on the back of the chair.

"Before Linda comes up, I want to share a few announcements. First, after Linda is finished sharing, you are free to go. I won't be sharing anything after Linda's talk. The second thing is that tomorrow's breakfast will be served between 6:30 and 7:30. You can rise early and have breakfast or sleep in a little and have breakfast later. And the last thing is that tomorrow we will be working in the fields again after breakfast, so dress accordingly."

Truth of Giving

"Now," Hank's face turned solemn, "Linda is going to share our last farmer's truth for tonight." Hank straightened up and slowly turned, making sure to catch everyone's eye. "This truth is not going to sit well with a lot of you. I'm warning you in advance. Hear her out."

"Linda, are you ready?"

Linda was already standing by the puzzle board. "Ready to give it my best," she cheerfully replied.

"Alright then, have at it."

"Dan and Kari, would you mind coming up here?" Linda asked quickly.

Dan and Kari glanced at each other. The look they gave was *why us?* Dan followed Kari up to the board.

"Thanks for volunteering—I know you didn't have much of a choice, but I appreciate it." Turning to Dan she said something to him that only the three of them could hear. Dan left them and headed to the whiteboard.

Linda handed a puzzle piece to Kari. "Kari, would you mind holding that piece up for everyone to see the word that is written on it?"

The Law Of The Seed

Kari complied and held up the piece, it read 'Giving'. "Good, now go ahead and place the piece within the puzzle." It took Kari a few seconds to figure out where the piece belonged. As soon as Kari had snapped the piece into place, Linda turned toward Dan who had just finished writing the truth on the whiteboard. It read, "Truth of Giving".

"Excellent. Thanks you two." Dan started to head back to his seat. "Not so fast, Dan," Linda stopped him mid-stride. "I still need you both."

Joe and Roger brought up three bar stools and placed them in the center, just in front of the dining tables.

"Perfect. Thanks Roger. Thanks Joe."

Linda directed Dan and Kari to sit alongside of her on the bar stools. Kari sat next to Linda on her left side and Dan sat on the other side of Kari.

Linda looked out at the group. "Well, it is kind of obvious what the last farmer's truth is for this evening. It's the 'Truth of Giving'."

Linda leaned forward a little on her bar stool, her feet dangling, unable to reach the floor. "The 'Truth of Giving' states that 'when you share and give of yourself to help others, you will be refreshed and blessed'."

"Now, I'm going to share with you why this is true. As you can see, I have asked Dan and Kari to help me.

"Now, don't be nervous. I'm going to ask you some simple questions that you already know the answer to. So it is not going to be tough at all."

Linda looked at Kari, "Kari, tonight you were picked to read the garden dedication to the kids. How did that make you feel?"

Kari looked at Linda. Kari's appearance changed almost instantly. Her eyes lit up and a smile appeared. "It felt great."

"Why did it feel great?"

Kari reflected on the question for a moment, "I don't know—I suppose it was because I knew that the food was really going to help feed them."

"You're right and…" Linda responded but was interrupted by Kari who was still deep in thought.

"And then when that young girl…" Kari's voiced cracked. Tears formed in her eyes. "When that young pregnant girl hugged me. That meant so much to me. I never thought that something so simple like sharing something like a garden would touch someone so much. I was a little overwhelmed."

Linda waited a few seconds to make sure that Kari was finished. Gently patting her back Linda whispered, "Thank you, Kari."

Linda turned a little on her bar stool to face Dan, who was sitting on the other side of Kari. "Dan, earlier this morning you were instrumental in helping the team lay out the planting plan. And then later we all planted the seeds based on that plan. How does that make you feel?"

Dan squirmed in this chair, not used to being the center of so much attention in one day. "Honestly Linda, it wasn't all me. The whole group helped."

"Dan I understand that, but you played a key role in laying out the best plan that I have seen so far. Knowing that you were able to help the whole team, how did that make you feel?"

"I felt…um…I felt…" Dan was struggling to come up with the right words.

"Valuable—Appreciated?" interjected Linda.

"Yah, I guess you can say that. I did feel valuable and like I was contributing something to the team. It kind of felt like the 'atta boy' I received from the guys on the team when I made a great tackle or blocked a punt. It felt good."

Linda stepped off of her bar stool and stood in front of it. Looking out at the group, "I can't explain it but giving from the heart and helping others—*feels* good. There is this satisfaction that comes in knowing that you personally did something to improve someone's life or in Dan's case, helping out the team."

Linda started to pace in front of the group as she talked. "I believe that God designed us to feel good when we help others unselfishly or without wanting something back, so that we would want to give. Does that make sense?" Linda asked.

"Speaking for Joe and myself, we just love to give and help. We have committed in our own lives, to give the first 10% of our harvest to our church. That harvest is our money, our time, our garden, among other things." Linda continued to pace, "and when we do, we feel good about ourselves…about our lives and what we are giving back."

Linda lowered her voice. "When Joe and I committed to giving…we *had* doubts. We didn't know how we were going to make our monthly budget. We had bills. But we wanted to give. So we did. Now I can't explain how but our monthly expenses were met. In fact, we had extra each month that we were able to apply to debt. Although we are not debt free yet, we will be in 32 months—and that includes our home."

"I know you have heard the saying, 'you reap what you sow'. I believe that. You *do* reap what you sow." Linda paused for the words to sink in.

"When the Ripple Group formed and we talked about starting up Ripple Farms with the Law of the Seed program, we committed to each other to give back. Tonight you all participated in one of our sowing projects. The Farmer's Truth of Giving is powerful. It will affect lives way beyond what you can imagine—and it *will* affect yours."

"I'm going to leave you with a couple of questions. I don't want to hear your answer. Just think about it. Here goes. What seeds are you planting? Do you want your life to be remembered as a taker or a giver? What are you reaping as a result of the seeds that you have sown so far in your life?"

Linda turned around and thanked Dan and Kari for helping. Linda walked past the group and joined her husband and the rest of the Ripple Farms' team as they left the barn, leaving the group by themselves.

No one said anything. One by one the group left. Jim and Jenny were left by themselves.

Jim was deeply impacted by everything that had taken place that evening. He wasn't ready for bed yet; he wanted to talk. "Jen, I'm not tired yet. Do you feel like sitting on the porch swing and talking?"

Jenny was a little surprised by Jim's request. He really never was the one that initiated the heart to heart talks, it usually was her. Although Jenny was tired, she agreed.

Jim found a swing away from the lights. With no lights nearby, it made the night sky look brighter. After a few minutes of gently swinging and gazing at the stars, Jim poured out his heart to Jenny.

"Jenny, I want us to change—I want to change. I don't want to keep doing what we have been doing. Even with all of the toys we have, I am still miserable and I know you are too. I want to be—I want *us* to be like Roger and Carolyn and be debt free and not worry about money. I want to help people. I want *us* to help people together."

The Law Of The Seed

Jenny leaned her head on Jim's shoulder and gently took Jim's hand with both of her hands and closed her eyes. *That is what I want too,* she thought. No words were necessary for Jim. He knew that Jenny agreed this too.

11
It Takes Water

> *Be sure to know the condition of your flocks.*
> *Give careful attention to your herds;*
> Proverbs 27:23

> *Opportunity is missed by most people because it is dressed in overalls and looks like work.*
> Thomas A. Edison
> 1847-1931, American Inventor, Scientist and Businessman

"Jenny?" Jim gently kissed Jenny on her forehead. "It's time to get up?" Jenny rolled over to see Jim standing next to the bed. "I'm going to get started."

Jenny slid out of bed, still half asleep and headed to the shower. *I need to do this.* She thought. *We need to do this together.* Prior to leaving the swing and heading to bed the night before, both of them had committed to each other to get up early each morning for as long as it took to work on their financial plan. It was 5:00 a.m.

For over an hour the two of them worked on the planning portion in the workbook. Together they had written out two of their five year goals and were starting on their third when they realized it was already 6:30. It was time for breakfast, and they were ready for it.

Both of them felt good at what they had accomplished that morning. Walking hand-in-hand into the barn, they were surprised to see that almost everyone was already there. There was quite a buzz in the air. Everyone was talking.

Jim and Jenny were warmly greeted by Ray who was planted at the end of the serving line, greeting everyone with his usual energetic 'good morning, farmers'. With their plates full, they made their way to the same seats as the night before.

The tables once again were decorated with colorful flowers and a card. The small card read, *"Be sure to know the condition of your flocks. Give careful attention to your herds;"* Proverbs 27:23

"All hard work brings a profit, but mere talk leads only to poverty." Proverbs 14:23

Interesting, Jim thought.

Jenny saw the sign also and was a little puzzled, "Jim, I'm not quite sure about the flocks and herd thing but I'm sure we are going to find out today."

"How are you guys this morning?" came a loud voice from behind Jim and Jenny.

Turning around, Jenny saw that it was Sharon, who from the looks of her plate was already done eating. "We're doing great," replied Jenny as she placed the napkin on her lap. "How are you doing, Sharon?"

"Believe it or not, I'm feeling great! I haven't felt like this in a long time." Sharon continued, not noticing that Jenny had just dropped a little scrambled egg on her lap. "I feel like I'm going to be okay—with the money part that is. Last night I couldn't go to sleep so I started reading the workbook. Have you guys started?"

This time Jenny's mouth was full, she just nodded.

"Well, that's good. I'm finding it very interesting. I never thought about setting financial goals. I don't think we ever thought about that. Last night I started to pencil in some goals. And believe it or not, the goals that I came up with all seem doable."

Realizing that her two new friends were trying to eat, "Hey, I'll stop jabbering so you two can eat."

Ray greeted the last two team members as they filled their plates. He was not surprised that everyone made it to breakfast before 7:00 even though they had 'til 7:30. The group was beginning to understand the importance of an early start.

Ray refilled his coffee mug, added some of his favorite flavored creamer and headed to the stage. Turning on the sound system, Ray checked the mic and then stood at the edge of the stage. "Well, this is our last day together," he began. "And let me tell you that it will be a fun filled day. Now I'm sure you are all wondering what we are going to do today. Well, I have decided…" Ray paused for a moment. "Not to tell you. Why change now? Life is more exciting when you don't know what to expect!"

"Now before we begin our day in the fields, I want to share a little devotion with you. I know that some of you are accustomed to going to church on Sundays, but since you are here with us today, you will not be able to. For those that don't attend church, don't worry, I'm not going to preach—instead I'm going to share a little story."

Ray walked down from the stage. "I need everyone to follow me outside just for a moment. Don't worry it won't be very long. Your coffee will still be warm when you get back."

Ray headed outside, across the drive and walked directly up to an old rusted out tractor which stood in the center of the circular gravel drive. The tractor was sitting on top of a patch of grass that looked like an oversized pitcher's mound.

The Law Of The Seed

Around the perimeter were brightly colored annuals in full bloom.

Jim and Jenny had ridden the farm chariot around the circle many times but never really noticed the tractor. Looking at it now, Jim knew why—it was really nothing to look at. The rubber was completely gone from the wheels. It was covered in rust and you couldn't even tell what color it was. The seat padding was gone and all that remained was the frame. It was in bad shape.

"Everyone get close so that you can hear me." The group moved closer to Ray. "I want to share a little story about this tractor and the barn. When Hank and Sue bought the farm, this tractor was found in one of the fields by their kids, completely covered with brush. Hank contacted the old owner and asked him about the tractor and what had happened."

Ray turned and touched the front of the tractor. "I know it is hard to see this emblem but it has an 'I' and an 'H' in it. This tractor was made by International Harvester and it was purchased in the summer of 1941 by the old farmer's father; it was the first of its kind in the whole county. He told Hank that his daddy loved this tractor. On Sundays he would invite people over for supper just to show off the tractor."

"His dad bought almost every attachment for this tractor that was possible in those days. The old farmer said it was during this time that he remembered his dad hardly spending any time with him or his brothers and sisters. Instead, he could always be found riding or working on the tractor. He told Hank it was not uncommon to find his Daddy repainting the tractor, so that it always looked new."

"The old farmer told him that he resented his Dad. When his Dad passed away, the old farmer decided to keep the tractor as a reminder to himself to not neglect his kids and focus on what is important."

"In the Bible there is a passage that says 'Do not store up for yourselves treasures on earth, where moth and rust destroy, and where thieves break in and steal. But store up for yourselves treasures in heaven, where moth and rust do not destroy, and where thieves do not break in and steal. For where your treasure is, there your heart will be also'."

"His dad's heart was on this treasure." Ray slapped the front of the tractor a couple of times to emphasize the point. "That treasure is all rust."

"When we formed the Ripple group and converted the farm, we did not want to do something that would turn to rust—we wanted to do something that would have lasting value—eternal value."

"If you guys would turn around, you will see what we did to the barn." The group turned around and looked at the red and white barn. "That barn needed major restoration, it used to look like the old tractor. Parts of the roof were missing, large support beams needed replacing. We decided to restore it because, unlike the rusted tractor, this barn would be a place where people would be encouraged. It would be a place where people would be educated about right principles–a place where they would be equipped to face life's challenges. Finally, it would be a place where we would evangelize the Harvest Principle, the Law of the Seed, and share our personal faith."

"Now if you look at the large columns that support the awning across the front of the barn you will see four words chiseled vertically–"

"I see it," shouted Maurice. "Encouraging, Educating, Equipping, Evangelizing!"

The Law Of The Seed

"Well, at least one person sees them," Ray responded jokingly. "Anyway, those words are there to remind me and the rest of the Ripple Team why we are here."

Ray moved to the front of the group. "Let me ask you a question. Will you be remembered as a tractor collector or a barn restorer?"

Ray paused, turned and looked at the barn. "You know how I want to be remembered."

Ray glanced at his watch. "Listen, in 30 minutes at 7:45 a.m. the farm chariot will here to pick you up. We'll see you then. You may go back and finish your breakfast." Ray walked away.

Jim turned to Jenny, "Be honest Jen. I'm a tractor collector, aren't I?"

Jenny reluctantly nodded.

"Well, that is going to change."

Just as Ray said, the farm chariot pulled up to the front of the barn. It was 7:45 a.m. sharp. Heather's voice came over the speakers, "Welcome everyone. Please... " Just then the music started, and Heather, along with her brother Caleb and two other boys, Chase and Hunter joined in. "... climb aboard, we're expecting you...The Love Boat soon will be making another run...The Love Boat promises something for everyone..." The voices faded away.

"It's great to have you all aboard the Ripple Farms only singing chariot. For your *non*-listening pleasure we have joining us today, Chase and Hunter, whose parents are Roger and Carolyn."

"Today, we have a short ride, so please take your seats, and as always, keep all fingers, toes and heads inside the chariot. Alright, I need your help in singing our next TV classic theme song. Here we go." The music and tractor roared to life and they were off singing to the theme song of the Brady Bunch.

Roger and Carolyn were sitting in their golf cart just in front of the group's newly planted garden when the chariot rounded the bend. They could hear the group singing "the Brady Bunch, that's the way we all became the Brady Bunch, the Brady Bunch." Roger and Carolyn both laughed. Carolyn turned to Roger, "I'm just so proud of the kids, making their job of being the farm's taxi service into something enjoyable and memorable for everyone."

The group pulled alongside Roger and Carolyn. All of them were wearing a smile and ready for the farming adventure that awaited them.

"Good morning everyone," Roger greeted the group. "It sounds like you all are having a great time singing."

"Of course we are," shouted Maurice. "Hey, we would've sounded better if it wasn't for the big guy singing," Maurice joked pointing at Dan. "I tried to help him—but, in his case, it's going to take a miracle."

Carolyn turned to Jim and Jenny who had just stepped off of the trailer. "I'm amazed that all of you still remember the lyrics after all these years."

"So am I," responded Jenny with a short laugh. "But I guess that if you watched the show as much as I did, you would remember it too."

Roger scanned the trailers to make sure everyone was off before continuing. "Well today is a new day—a great day for learning."

"Yesterday, you all learned the first three principles of the Law of the Seed—and those were?" Roger looked at Jim. "Jim?"

"Plan, prepare and plant," answered Jim.

The Law Of The Seed

"Good. Thanks, Jim. Now does everyone understand the relationship of those three farming principles to finances?" The group nodded in unison.

"Great. Well today, we are going to share the next principle. It's not a complicated principle – in fact I would say that 100% of all farmers never miss this step and neither will you when you plant a garden. To prove my point, I am going to let you tell me the next principle."

"Where is Kari?" Roger asked looking around.

"I'm here, Roger," replied Kari nervously.

"Kari, why don't you come over here and stand between Carolyn and me. Don't worry—I know you can do this."

Kari made her way to Roger and Carolyn. "Kari, have you ever planted a garden before?"

"No, never. I never even planted a flower."

"Perfect. Now let me ask you…" Roger stopped mid—sentence and turned from Kari and looked at the group. "Before I ask Kari the question, please don't shout out any answers. I want you to hear her answer and to prove my point."

Roger turned back to Kari, "Now Kari, yesterday you helped plan the garden. You and the rest of the team helped prepare the field for the seeds. And then you planted the seeds. Now here is the million dollar question; for the seed to grow what secret ingredient does it need?"

Kari smiled and thought to herself, *this is too easy. It must be a trick question.* "This is not a trick question is it?"

"No, it isn't Kari. Come on. You know the answer."

"Well, it needs water… and…" Kari paused for a moment, looking at her husband and then back at Roger, "it also needs the sun."

It Takes Water

Roger didn't answer right away. He looked at the group. "By raising your hands, how many people agree with Kari that the next thing the seed needs is water?"

Everyone raised their hands including Roger and Carolyn. "Well Kari—you're right. Good job. I was sure you would know the answer."

Roger turned his attention back to the group. "Yesterday, when I was talking with Dan and Kari, she shared that she never planted anything—ever. So I thought she would be perfect for today's session. You see, you don't have to be a full-time farmer to understand some of these principles, some of it is common sense."

"Now Kari said something else that no one has ever said before to me. She mentioned another ingredient—the sun."

Turning back to Kari Jim asked, "Kari, why did you mention the sun?"

Kari was now a little confused. Thinking to herself, *Roger just said that no one ever mentioned this to him before. So it must have been a stupid comment. I know I'm not that smart.* "I don't know," she half-whispered.

Roger looked at Kari, "I think you do know. Come on – think about it."

Kari was silent for a moment. She looked over the garden, then she looked at her husband trying to read his face for the answer. *Think it through.* "The seeds need the sun to grow—they need the light."

"Sort of," Roger responded. Being careful not to make her feel any more insecure asked, "What does the light produce?"

"Heat?" she answered, unsure if that was the answer he was looking for.

"Yes, that's it. If the seeds only needed light then we should be able to shine flashlights on the ground and the

The Law Of The Seed

seeds would grow. But that doesn't happen. Also, in the winter time, the sun is out but nothing grows. Why? Because it's too cold. The seed needs to feel the warmth of the sun."

"Everyone, pay attention to Carolyn as she explains this more."

Carolyn held up a glass jar. It was a canning jar that was filled with dirt. "I'm going to pass around some jars. Take a minute and look at it and then pass it around." Carolyn passed out a dozen jars.

Jim and Jenny looked at their jar. They could barely make out the seed but it looked like there was a little sprout coming out of the seed.

"What you all are looking at is a process known as germination. Seeds grow when they have both moisture and warm soil present. As farmers it is our responsibility to make sure we provide these two ingredients after we plant, if we want the seeds to grow. 'Provide' is the next principle of the Law of the Seed."

Carolyn removed a small whiteboard from the back of the golf cart and wrote down 'Provide' on the line after 'Plant'.

The	**PLAN**	+
Law	**PREPARE**	+
Of	**PLANT**	+
The	**PROVIDE**	+
Seed	_____	+

Joy raised her hand and, before Carolyn could call on her, she asked her question. "You just said that the next principle is 'Provide'. I know that we can provide moisture by turning on the water hose but how do we provide warmth—we just can't turn on the sun, we're not God?"

"You're right Joy—we are not God. But we do have some control. For example, we wouldn't plant seeds in the winter because the soil would be too cold but we would plant them in the spring when it's warmer outside. Or we could choose to plant the seeds inside our home or a greenhouse where we could control the temperature. Does that make sense, Joy?" Joy nodded her head.

"I have one more point that I would like to make before Roger shows you how we are going to water the garden. With providing, comes understanding. You must have understanding—a knowledge of how much to provide. Too much of a good thing can damage or even kill the seed. Can you imagine what would happen if we provided too much water? The seed would drown. Or if we would plant the seed in the dead of summer when the ground is hot? The seed would die. We need understanding."

Roger stepped forward. "We have a number of hoses here, along with sprinklers. Let's go ahead and lay them out and attach the oscillating sprinklers to them."

The group grabbed the hoses, uncoiled them and laid them along the ground. A few of the guys attached the sprinklers to them. It didn't take long for the group to have sprinklers laid throughout the garden.

"Alright, what we need to do is attach these hoses to these timers and the timers to the hose bibs. The reason we are adding timers is that I don't like to stand around for 30 minutes before turning off the water. These timers will do that for us. In fact, we can even program the timers to water at certain times of the day. I have already programmed them to water early in the morning and in the evening for 30 minutes each time. Watering when it is cooler is better because the water won't evaporate as much."

"Let's go ahead and attach these."

The Law Of The Seed

Soon everything was attached and ready for watering. Roger had Jim walk over to one side of the garden and turned on the water. The group watched. It was obvious after a couple of rotations of the sprinkler that it was not reaching one side of the garden. Roger motioned for Jim to move the sprinkler while it was still running.

"I bet you a dollar that he gets wet," Maurice challenged the group. Jenny looked at Maurice who had a mischievous grin on his face.

"You're on, Maurice Baby," she replied, accepting his challenge.

The group watched Jim dart out to the sprinkler, jumping over the marked rows of seeds. As he got close, the sprinkler was just about ready to soak him. Suddenly, Jim reached down and grabbed the hose and bent it in half, pinching off the flow of water. He then moved the sprinkler to the edge another ten feet. Releasing the hose, the sprinkler sprang to life, watering the furthest side just as it was needed. Jim jumped back over the rows and raced back to the edge so not to get caught in the steady stream of water. He made it.

Jenny snatched the dollar bill from Maurice's hand who now had a large grin on her face. "Pleasure doing business with you." The group roared with laughter.

Jim continued turning one sprinkler on at a time and setting them in place so that all areas were covered by the gentle stream of falling water. Soon the garden was blanketed by a steady rain of water. Jim headed back to rejoin the group.

"Well done Jim," congratulated Roger. "You are pretty quick on your feet." Roger raised his voice a little so that the group could hear him above the sound of the sprinklers that were oscillating all across the garden.

"Does everyone see how the sprinklers are evenly watering the garden? When watering freshly planted seeds, you want to make sure that you are not over watering and that you are not pouring large amounts of water on the soil. This may wash away the soil and expose the seed or even wash away the seed themselves."

"Well, we are done here. But I do want to take you to another garden for a few minutes. Just follow that path through the trees. It's about a hundred yards down that path. Carolyn and I will meet you over there."

The group headed down the trail. Roger and Carolyn collected the seed jars, placed them in the back of their golf cart, and started down the path.

The trail led to a clearing where there was another garden the same size as theirs. The garden was planted some time ago. The corn stalks were about five feet tall, tomatoes could be seen on the plants, and cucumbers were forming along the ground. The garden was well on its way.

Roger and Carolyn arrived in the golf cart. Roger slid out and walked over to the group. "As you all can see, this garden was planted some time ago. In about another month or so it will be ready to harvest. Now this garden has a little problem. As farmers, we're to provide. Remember 'provide' is the fourth principle of the Law of the Seed. Now if you look at the ground and the leaves of the plants, what do you see?"

Jim noticed that only part of the ground was wet, but before he could respond to Roger's question, Sharon blurted out "weeds."

"That is not exactly what I am looking for Sharon. Keep looking."

"Roger, I see that only part of the garden is getting watered," Jim responded.

The Law Of The Seed

"Now why is that Jim?"

Jim looked over the garden to see how they were being watered. Sure enough there were two sprinklers in particular that were hidden behind the growing stalks of corn.

Jim pointed to the two sprinklers, "I would say that those sprinklers are being blocked by the corn."

"You're right, Jim. We need to raise those tripod sprinklers up at least a couple of feet." Roger turned to the group. "Do I have a volunteer to adjust those sprinklers?"

"I'll do it!" Maurice exclaimed. "But only if I can get a chance to win my dollar back?"

Jenny curiously looked at Maurice, "So what did you have in mind?"

"I'll bet you, double or nothing, that I can adjust those two sprinklers without getting wet."

Jenny, sensing that Maurice was trying to pull a fast one over her responded, "Maurice, I may be a blonde, but why would I accept that offer when the sprinklers are not even running?"

"Jenny, come on—I had to try."

"Listen Maurice, I know you hated losing to me, a woman and all, but I am willing to give you a chance to get even with me."

"I'm listening."

"I challenge you to a sprinkler dual. With those two sprinklers on, the first person who can raise their sprinkler and return back to this spot without getting wet is the winner. And the loser has to serve dinner to the winner."

"Oh, you are on. I accept your challenge but with one slight change." responded Maurice enthusiastically.

"And what *slight change* would that be?"

"If I win then all of the ladies serve the guys dinner."

"And if *I* win the guys will serve the ladies." Jenny looked at all of the ladies in the group. "What do you gals think?" Everyone started to clap and cheer. Jenny turned to Maurice, "We accept your wager."

Jenny sat on the ground and removed her shoes and socks.

"That ain't going to help you, Blondie," needled Maurice. Maurice turned to the guys. "You guys with me?" Now all of the guys were hollering and whistling.

The group split. The ladies lined up behind Jenny and the guys all grouped around Maurice.

This is not what Roger had planned, but he thought it would be fun to watch. He went over and turned on the two sprinklers and then walked over to Jenny and Maurice. "Listen you two. To raise the sprinkler, all you do is pull the pin out just above the tripod and slide the tube up and re-insert the pin. And just be careful not to step on the vegetables. You guys ready?"

"Alright, on your mark, get set and go!" shouted Roger.

Maurice was off quickly. Jenny had to wait for the sprinkler to pass. Maurice jumped over a couple of rows of vegetables and then he had to stop and wait for the sprinkler to pass. Jenny caught up and together they reached the tripods at the same time.

Jenny struggled with the pin. It took some strength to pull out the pin. Maurice just gave a couple of tugs and his was out. But with the pins out both of them found that raising the sprinkler was not as easy as they had thought. Jenny found that she could not pull up on the sprinkler and set the pin at the same time. She stopped for a moment and looked at the tripod. Then she had an idea, she removed her belt from her jeans.

The Law Of The Seed

Maurice found that he too could not raise the sprinkler up with one hand so he darted around looking for a log, a branch, anything that he could brace underneath the tripod tube to hold it into position.

Jenny wrapped her belt around the pipe twice and raised the sprinkler. As she raised the sprinkler she slid the belt down against the tripod base. The belt caused enough friction to hold the sprinkler in place. After a couple of adjustments she was able to slide the pin in place.

Although Jenny's method was pretty inventive, Maurice's basic use of propping a stick under the sprinkler was quick and effective. Maurice was already running back to the group before Jenny started running. Fortunately for Jenny, Maurice had to stop to avoid the sprinkler from hitting him.

Maurice, seeing that victory was just a couple dozen feet away, turned around and started taunting Jenny. Jenny raced on—jumping over the last couple of rows of vegetables. Maurice turned around to complete the race but instead found himself right in the middle of the cucumber patch. Trying to avoid further damaging the plants, Maurice jumped. It was too late. With his foot caught in one of the vines, he was unable to maintain his balance and fell face forward onto the wet ground. Jenny finished, to the delight of her supporters.

Jenny looked back just in time to catch Maurice getting drenched by the passing sprinkler. Maurice, realizing he lost, stood up, and slowly walked up to Jenny with his arms outstretched. "I would like to give you a congratulatory hug." Jenny pushed him away and held out her hand. Maurice shook.

Still trying to recover from his embarrassing defeat, Maurice looked around and then raised his hands to quiet the group. "Folks, I want to share one thing with you. What I demonstrated here in true classic form, is the Farmer's Truth of Focus. Setting out to demonstrate this concept from the very beginning, you can see that if you, as a financial farmer, take your eyes off of the goal—you will lose. I hope—"

"Thank you Maurice," interrupted Roger by patting him on the back. "I think you better stop while you are still ahead."

"Maurice, I do have a question for you. Would you say that this garden needs more water or less water than your freshly planted garden?" Roger asked trying to get the group back on track.

"It needs more water because everything is growing."

"Exactly. As farmers we need to make sure we provide what the vegetables need in order to flourish and provide a bountiful harvest."

"I know that Maurice was joking about demonstrating the Truth of Right Focus but folks, that's what's needed when you practice the principle of provide. You must focus on what the seed needs and all the stages of its growth, if you want to experience a harvest."

Kari raised her hand and started waving it back and forth to get Roger's attention.

"Yes, Kari."

"Roger, I'm just a little confused about 'providing'. I understand that seeds need water to grow but how do we provide for our money when our money is supposed to provide for us? I just don't get it."

Roger looked at her and smiled. "Great question Kari, I was hoping that someone would ask that question. Let me see if I can help you answer that for yourself by walking you through an example. First, let me ask you, what is our seed this weekend?"

The Law Of The Seed

Kari quickly replied, "Money."

"You're right. Money – finances is our seed." Roger reached into his pocket and pulled out a dollar bill. "This is our seed. Now Kari, what is the purpose of this seed?"

"To pay for things?" Kari answered, a little unsure of her answer.

"Not quite Kari," responded Roger as he walked to the center of the group. Squatting down, he took the dollar bill and poked it into the ground, so that only a portion of it was visible.

"Kari, this dollar bill is the seed, I just planted it. By planting it, we are expecting it to…?"

"Grow!"

"You're right – we want it to grow. Because when it grows it will…? Roger hesitated again, wanting Kari to provide the answer.

"Harvest – it will produce a Harvest," Kari replied confidently.

"Exactly! Now, what can we use the harvest for?"

Kari looked at Roger, unsure if she should repeat her earlier answer. "Pay for things."

"Now you are getting it. The harvest—the money generated from our seed, can be used to pay for daily living expenses, pay off debt, fund our retirement or whatever you had planned."

Roger reached into his pocket and pulled out more money. "Kari, what do personally do to generate a harvest of money?" Roger asked as he thumbed through the bills.

"Well, I make and sell jewelry."

"That's pretty interesting. Well, if you wanted to have a large harvest you would have to…?" Roger paused.

"Sell more jewelry."

"And to sell more jewelry, you would have to make more. And to make more jewelry, what would you need to do?"

Kari thought for a second, "I would need more supplies, like beads, clasps, and wire."

Roger nodded his head in agreement, "You're right. You would need more supplies. And that takes money. So for every $1 you *invest* for supplies, your harvest will be how much?"

"Depending on the type of jewelry, I would make somewhere between $6 and $8."

Roger counted out $8 and gave it to Kari. Holding up a dollar bill, he continued with his example. "Your seed is really your jewelry business and by providing two main ingredients which are…? Roger pointed to his watch and waved the dollar bill.

Kari answered, "Time and money."

"Exactly. You are providing—investing time and money to make the seed grow. Now, if you did not provide some money for supplies or invest some of your personal time, what would happen to your seed?"

"My business would fail," replied Kari as her expression changed. "I get it. I understand the 'Provide Principle' now."

As Kari handed the money back to Roger, she continued talking. "Whatever our seed is to make money, we need to make sure that we provide everything we can so that it continues to make us money."

"You're absolutely right," answered Roger. "If someone's main financial seed is their job, they need to water it—invest in it. That may require taking additional educational courses to make you more valuable. Or it may

The Law Of The Seed

be as simple as doing your best—giving 100% to your employer while you are working."

Roger folded up the money and placed it in his pocket. "Remember everyone, the harvest principle says 'The seed is the future. Take care of the seed and the seed will take care of you.' You need to take care of your main financial seed."

Roger glanced at his watch, "Well, we need to be moving on to the next session, which is learning about your last principle from the Law of the Seed. Joe and Linda are expecting you. So if you all would just take that trail and follow the signs, it will lead you to Joe and Linda." Roger pointed to a small clearing between two oak trees.

12
The Challenge Trail

> *What is the difference between an obstacle and an opportunity? Our attitude towards it. Every opportunity has a difficulty and every difficulty has an opportunity.*
> J. Sidlow Baxter
> 1903-1999, Minister, Theologian

Suspended high above the trail, an engraved wooden sign read "Ripple Farms Challenge Trail". As the group approached the mouth of the trail, another sign staked in the ground was viewable.

Warning:
Challenges Await To Those That Enter
Must Have Knowledge Of The Law Of The Seed
Do Not Enter Alone
Teamwork A Must
Enter At Your Own Risk

"Oh, this is too cool!" shouted Maurice enthusiastically as he darted down the path.

Jim and Jenny walked with Dan and Kari behind the rest of the group. If this was a true challenge, both couples wanted to make sure that they took their time to read and observe everything on the trail.

More signs littered the trail. "Plan", "Prepare", "Plant" and "Provide" were mounted on four-by-four posts just above the ground; spaced about 50 feet apart.

Just as the group passed the last sign, Jim decided to look back at the trail. At first glance he saw nothing. As he was

The Law Of The Seed

turning around his eye caught something just behind the sign – something white.

"Hey Guys, wait a sec," Jim shouted to the group as he headed back to the last sign with Dan following him. Kneeling down, he found a folded piece of paper stapled to the back of the wooden sign.

Dan knelt beside him. "What does it say?"

Jim unfolded the piece of paper only to find a picture. "It doesn't say anything." Jim held out the paper to show Dan. "It looks like a stick figure standing on something."

"That's strange," responded Dan after looking at the hand drawn picture. "I wonder if there are more of these on the other signs? I'm going to take a look." Dan rose quickly to his feet and jogged back to the previous signs.

"Hey Jen!" Jim yelled cupping his hands around his mouth.

Jenny turned around to see Jim standing up. "Tell the group to come back."

Everyone gathered around Jim, except for Maurice who was long gone. Jim held up the paper for the group to see. "Hey I found more drawings," exclaimed Dan as he jogged back to the group. "I even found one behind the very first sign."

Jim took the first piece and held it up for the group to see. It showed what appeared to be a river with a bridge going over it. The bridge had an "X" thru it.

The next piece of paper showed three stick figures standing next to this river but now it had no bridge.

Jenny spoke up. "This trail must lead us to a river or a creek—or something like that. The bridge is out. I bet you that the next picture will show that we have to build something to cross it."

The Challenge Trail

Jim unfolded the next one, which came from behind the "prepare" sign. Sure enough it showed two long rectangular shapes and two "Ts" with a plus sign in between them and then another plus sign with a picture of a hammer.

"Yes it's showing us to build something. Those rectangles could be wood and the "Ts" are nails. We are supposed to build a bridge to cross the river," Jenny shouted excitedly.

The next picture showed two squiggly lines with pictures of the rectangles, nails and hammer spread evenly along the lines.

"I think those are showing us that what we need is along the trail," blurted Kari, pointing to the paper that Jim was holding.

"I think you ladies are right," responded Jim, holding up the first piece of paper he found. "Then this picture must show us crossing the river."

"Good job Jim," exclaimed Dan. "Let's keep our eyes open."

The group headed down the trail excitedly. Not long after they passed the last sign someone found a hammer and another found a plastic bag with nails hidden under a patch of leaves. Rounding a sharp turn on the trail the group spotted two really long planks, approximately ten inches wide and about twenty feet long.

Grabbing the wooden planks, the group now had everything that the pictures had shown. The group continued on. The trail made a couple of "S" turns and then straightened out, rising up a small hill. At the crest of the small hill, the group spotted Maurice lying on the ground just ahead of them. Fearing the worst, some ran down the hill to him, shouting his name.

The Law Of The Seed

"What took you so long?" Maurice questioned as he stood up brushing the leaves and grass from his pants and shirt.

"Maurice Everett Johnson!" Joy pushed through the group slapping him across his arm. "Why did you scare us like that?"

"Hey Babe, I was just resting. I didn't mean to scare you." Maurice tried to hug Joy but she resisted.

"Take a look at this – this will scare you," Maurice stepped up to the edge of a small creek.

The creek was about ten feet below them, flowing quickly past the rocks. The embankment was about the same distance away from where the trail continued.

"I'm not sure how we are going to cross this using only this rope." Maurice held up a thick sized rope.

"We're not," responded Jim as he knelt down at the edge of the small ledge. "Alright everyone, let's get to work."

The group laid the two planks on top of one another and nailed them together. Maurice watched, wondering how they knew to bring the planks and questioning where they found the nails and hammer.

Dan answered Maurice, "In your rush to get here, you passed the signs that had clues stapled to them, and you passed up all of the supplies that we needed to get over the creek."

Joy, still upset with Maurice, saw an opportunity to express her feelings. "Maurice, you are always racing into things without thinking. Doing this, and doing that, a lot of times without even asking me. That is why we are having money trouble—because you don't think. Everything is a joke to you."

Maurice withdrew from the group, feeling completely humiliated by his wife's public scolding.

The Challenge Trail

Jenny put her arm around Joy who was trembling. Jim looked at Dan, both of them unsure what to do about Maurice, as they continued working on the plank.

"Alright Team," Jim said. "Now it's time to place our new bridge into position. Dan and I will hold the bottom down while you all lift the top and flip it over the creek. Ready?"

The group lifted the end, standing the plank straight up. Then with a push the plank fell across the creek, like a tree falling after it had been cut by a lumberjack. Jim and Dan held firm to the end as it tried to bounce up after the other end hit the ground.

The group cheered as the plank reached the other side. "Now we have a bridge," someone shouted.

Jim turned to Dan, "I know what the last picture means now. It shows a stick figure crossing the plank, but it also shows it hanging on to something. That's what the rope is for—to protect."

"Yah, you're right Jim. That makes sense." Dan grabbed the rope, "I'm going to cross first and I will tie one end off on one of those trees over there."

"And I will tie the other end off here," Jim responded. "Hey by you going first, being the big guy and all, if the boards can hold you, then we know it can support us."

The group watched as Dan inched his way across the board. It didn't take long before Dan and Jim had the rope tied off. Jenny volunteered to go next. Like a pro she walked across the board barely using the rope to support herself.

Ten minutes later the group was across and they were heading down the trail. After about a hundred yards they came to the end of the trail and were greeted by a sign that read:

The Law Of The Seed

Congratulations Farmers
You Planned
You Prepared
You Planted
You Protected Each Other
and...
You Succeeded!

13
To Protect

Discretion will protect you,
and understanding will guard you.
Proverbs 2:11

Energy and persistence conquer all things.
Benjamin Franklin
1706-1790, American Statesman, Author, Inventor

"Congratulations you guys—you've set a trail record," Joe enthusiastically repeated as the team members exited from the challenge trail. "Head over to where Linda. She has some food and drinks for you." Joe directed the group, pointing to the shady area just beyond the garden.

Linda handed out ice cold sodas and water bottles, along with fresh cut watermelon and sandwiches, as the team sat down on the grass.

Joe walked up carrying a shoe box. "Before Linda shares the last principle of the Law of the Seed, we have something that we want to give you on behalf of all of us, at Ripple Farms." Joe pulled out a navy blue bandana and began to fold it over and over again. "This is an official Ripple Farms body cooler. Believe me, you are going to need this today—being so hot and all. All you do is fold it like this, pour cold water on it, and tie it around your neck. It will keep you feeling cool..."

The Law Of The Seed

"And looking cool," interjected Linda. "Well, like Joe said, I will be sharing about the last principle of the Law of the Seed."

Linda held up a small white board and wrote "Protect", on the last line.

The	**PLAN**	+
Law	**PREPARE**	+
Of	**PLANT**	+
The	**PROVIDE**	+
Seed	**PROTECT**	+

"One of the toughest jobs for a farmer is protecting the crop. The farmer has animals, bugs, disease, and weather to contend with. All of these can be devastating to the garden. If the farmer is not diligent, he could be faced with no harvest. Let me show you what I'm talking about with this garden here." Linda headed over to the garden as the group followed.

She knelt down on one knee. "Take a look at these carrots and the lettuce behind me. What do you see?"

"It looks like something has been eating them," answered Jenny.

"You're right Jenny. Wild rabbits have been eating these vegetables. As farmers we need to protect our garden. So what do you all suggest we do?"

"Put up a scarecrow—or does that only work for birds?" suggested Sharon.

"That doesn't work for rabbits but that is something you may want to consider to scare away the birds that have been eating the corn in the garden."

"I would put up a fence," suggested Dan, "just a simple one, like a chicken wire fence."

"Perfect. That's exactly what we were planning on doing. Before we build a fence, let's take a look at the tomatoes; I noticed some worm damage."

Linda showed the tomato damage to the group. "To help fight off the hornworms, we are going to use an all natural pesticide to spray the leaves with."

"Alright, the spray and the fence will take care of the bugs and animals—what else do you farmers see that is hurting the garden?"

"Some of the corn looks like they have been eaten," commented Sharon. "So I think we need a scarecrow built to scare off the birds."

"Sounds good, Sharon. I think I will put you in charge of the scarecrow," responded Linda.

"What else do you see? Let me give a hint. This *thing* is hurting the growth of the plants."

"I see weeds, everywhere," responded Jim, pulling up a handful and showing Linda.

"Jim, you are exactly right. There are weeds everywhere. Weeds stump the vegetables' growth by choking out the vegetable roots, they use the same nutrients that the vegetables need to grow, and they steal water from the plants."

Linda pointed to a row of plants. "See this row here?" These were seeds planted from the seed bag that had no name on them. These are all weeds! And these weeds grew so quickly that their seeds infected the other parts of the garden."

Turning to Jim and Jenny, "I believe you guys had the same bag of seed and you prevented the group from planting the seeds. Good job. If you hadn't done that then your garden would look like this."

"So farmers, how do we get rid of weeds?" asked Linda.

The Law Of The Seed

"We pull them out!" someone shouted.

"You're absolutely right."

Linda motioned for Joe to come over. "Alright farmers, now it's time to get to work. I will be taking the ladies with me and we are going to work on the scarecrow and apply some pesticide. Joe is going to take the guys and you are going to build the fence. Then whenever we get done, we all are going to start weeding. Alright, let's get to work."

The guys followed Joe to one corner of the garden, where he challenged them to apply the Law of the Seed to fence building. So the guys applied what they had learned. They first created a plan, which involved having two of them unroll the chicken wire; then another would rotate the fence up so that the next person could weave the stake through the chicken wire; the last guy would drive the stake into the ground. They formed two teams.

The second principle was to prepare. So both teams of men gathered the tools they needed, then the stakes and the fencing, laying everything out.

Then they planted; they put their plan into action. It didn't take long for the guys to completely fence off the entire one acre garden.

After the fence was staked into place, they added a pair of gates, one on each end.

Most of the guys were impressed with Joe's challenge. They had no idea that the Law of the Seed would not only apply to finances but would apply to something as simple as fence building. Jim was particularly impressed—stating to himself that he should apply this to his job.

Linda also challenged the ladies to apply the Law of the Seed to building the scarecrow. Linda had Sharon lead the group. The ladies planned what the scarecrow was going to look like, the height, the material from which it was going to be made and where it would be located. They then gathered the supplies. Once the supplies were all located, they began to build the scarecrow.

When the scarecrow was completed, they planted it right in front of the corn field. They provided and protected the scarecrow with a few bells and sealed off the sleeves so that the field mice would not be tempted to take some of the straw and make a home with it. Like the fence, building the scarecrow did not take long.

Weeding proved more difficult for everyone. There were weeds everywhere. Although most of the vegetable plants were larger than the weeds, the group still had to be careful not to pull the vegetable plants out with the weeds. The rows in between the vegetables were weeded by using a garden hoe.

After working hard for over an hour, the garden was weed free. "You guys did a great job," Joe praised. "Just take a look at the garden; the fence is up. We have a pretty scarecrow guarding the corn in a dress—why, I will never know—"

"It's because the dress will flutter in the wind which tends to scare off the birds—pants don't flutter," responded Sharon defensively.

"Live and learn. Thanks Sharon for teaching me something new. Anyway, you guys also sprayed for bugs and pulled weeds. To protect is hard work."

"But I will tell you, as you grow more and more gardens, planning in advance for protecting your garden becomes easier."

Dan was a little puzzled by Joe's statement. "Joe, I'm not sure I understand what you mean about planning in advance for protecting your garden. How can you plan in advance for weeds and bugs—you will always have them?"

The Law Of The Seed

"Great question Dan." Looking at the rest of the group, Joe continued, "I'm sure a lot of you are thinking the same thing. But there are ways to significantly reduce weeds in your garden, but it takes advanced planning. Let me show you what I mean."

Joe walked over to the edge of the garden. "Do you remember how many weeds were in between the rows of vegetables—there were a lot. Well, one thing that you can do is plan in advance to apply mulch to those areas. With two to four inches of mulch, sunlight is not able to penetrate and, as a result, weeds have a hard time growing. You can also use black plastic in between the rows. Plastic or a weed fabric prevents weeds from growing."

"Let me share another method. Just like the vegetables, weeds need water to grow. Another option to reduce weed growth is by *not* watering the entire garden area. Right now the sprinklers that we have set up, water the entire acre. We are watering both the vegetables and the weeds. What we could do is plan in advance to run a drip-irrigation along the vegetable rows only. That way we are not watering the entire lot but only the vegetables."

"Do you see how planning protection in advance is possible?"

The group nodded their heads in agreement.

"Just as we can plan in advance to protect our garden from weeds, bugs, and animals, we also need to protect our finances. Let me tell you what I mean."

"Looking back at our lives, both Linda and I made some really dumb decisions. One of our biggest, as Linda shared at the Imagine Circle, was buying all of those toys and going into debt, big-time. What she didn't share, was the one smart thing we did—protecting our financial seeds."

To Protect

"Early on in our marriage, we learned that weeds could choke the growth of our money. One type of weed, which you are all familiar with, is called taxes. Now don't get me wrong, we need to pay taxes but *only* what is required. We discovered that we could reduce our tax burden by itemizing our deductions. We contributed to our 401(k) and IRA which reduced our adjusted gross income—the amount that determines your tax rate. I don't want to get into a lot of detail, but I just want to make a point that there are things you can do legally to protect your hard earned money from the Tax Weed. Sometimes it pays to hire a Tax Weed expert, like an Accountant, that can help you protect your garden, if you know what I mean?"

"Another example..." Joe began. Just then the sound of two horn blasts coming from the approaching farm chariot, interrupted the talk.

"What timing," Joe commented sarcastically. Turning back to the distracted group, "Stay with me farmers, I have one more important thing that I need to share."

Joe walked over to the newly installed fence and stood by the gate. "Linda and I never built a fence around our finances, until much later in our lives. Just like the guys installed a fence to keep the animals out of the garden, Linda and I realized that we needed to protect our money by installing a fence around our financial garden. That fence we called a Cash Flow Plan. You may know it as a budget."

"You see, we discovered that our money was disappearing and we really didn't understand how or where it was going. So we drafted up a cash flow plan."

"With our cash flow plan, we assigned every dollar into different categories; like housing, food, transportation, and insurance. Each category had an amount and we followed that plan, making sure that we did not spend more than we had budgeted. And it worked."

"We noticed, almost immediately, that our financial harvest did not disappear without us knowing about it." Joe opened the small gate, closed it and then opened it again. "You see, we built the fence and a gate. Our harvest only left when we opened the gate. You guys follow me?"

Again the group nodded their head.

"Good." Joe turned his attention to the chariot that was parked. "Well, I guess they're ready for you. But before you leave, do you have any questions for Linda or me?"

Jim raised his hand. "Yes Jim."

Jim stood to his feet. "For the last three plus hours we have worked hard on another team's garden. Is there anyway, that we can go back to our garden and protect it by adding a fence, mulch in between our rows and adding a drip irrigation system—?" Jenny tugged on Jim's pant leg and whispered "scarecrow". "Oh, and add a scarecrow?"

"You guys just blow me away," Joe responded. "No one has ever asked to go back to their planted garden and protect it in advance!"

Linda spoke up. "Jim, we appreciate your willingness to go back to protect your garden but we are going to have the next group that comes through the program do that. We need to have something for them to do."

"Well, if that's the case. Maybe they can do a little extra and add the mulch and the drip-irrigation to it. It will be interesting to come back and see how well it worked."

"I think that's a great idea Jim—you have my word," replied Joe.

"Well, you guys better get going because I believe that Hank and Sue are expecting you."

"See you all later."

To Protect

One by one the team of farmers made their way on to the chariot.

14
Truth Of Forgiveness

To err is human, to forgive, divine.
Alexander Pope
1688-1744, English Poet

"Please remain seated," sounded Heather over the intercom. "We are going to stop for just a second and pick up these two hitch hikers."

Jim was lost in his observation of Maurice and Joy, completely unaware that Hank and Sue were the two hitch hikers that Heather was referring to.

It was obvious to Jim that Maurice was not himself and was still upset with Joy at what she had said on the trail. Maurice was sitting on the edge of his seat looking away from Joy, even though she was trying to get his attention. *I wonder if there is something that I can do,* Jim thought to himself.

"Jim?" Hank repeated for the third time. "Jim, how are you doing?"

Jim snapped out of his trance. "I'm sorry Hank—I was just thinking. I'm doing fine. I—."

Hank motioned to Jenny to switch seats. Jenny obliged. "What's on your mind, Jim?" Hank asked slowly looking into the direction that Jim was staring.

"It's really nothing Hank."

Pushing a little more, Hank continued, "Jim, I don't believe you—." Hank still looking at the direction that Jim was staring, "Does it have to do with Maurice?"

Reluctantly Jim answered, "Yes, it does—those two had an argument back on the trail. Some things were said that really hurt Maurice." Jim paused for a moment and looked at Hank. "I know how he feels."

"Being confronted with the truth sometimes hurts. Jim, have you had a chance to talk with Maurice?"

"No. It's really not my place."

"I have to disagree, Jim. It *is* your place. It is your place to come along side of him and encourage him and tell him that you can relate. It's not your place to judge or choose sides."

"There is a passage in Proverbs that says, 'As iron sharpens iron, so one man sharpens another.'"

"I—I don't understand what you mean, Hank."

"Jim, I have always taken that little saying to mean to be better—to have a sharper mind, it's good to have a friend that will come up and challenge you without breaking you. Sometimes it's easier to hear your shortcomings from a friend rather than your spouse."

"Hank, I agree with you there." Jim looked away and then at Maurice. His eyes were downcast and the smirk that he always had on his face was gone. "Thanks Hank, I think I *will* talk to him."

"Sounds good Jim. Look, we are almost here."

"Where's here?" asked Jim looking around only noticing an approaching garden.

Pointing to the garden, "That's it, Jim. That's our harvest."

Hank reached behind him and took the mic from his daughter's hand. "Farmers, we are here. See that garden over there?" Hank pointed to the approaching garden. The tractor began to throttle back. "This garden is ready to be harvested—and we are going to harvest."

The Law Of The Seed

"When you get off, Sue and I are going to hand you a basket to fill up. Please fill your basket with only one type of vegetable. As soon as you're done, just bring your basket back to the chariot."

Jim saw this as his opportunity to talk to Maurice who was heading off by himself to the far end of the garden. Quickly informing Jenny of his plan, he dashed off to catch up with Maurice. Jenny joined Joy and the two of them went to another area of the garden.

Jim caught up with Maurice and walked along beside him, not saying a word. Maurice started to pull off the ears of corn and toss them into the basket, missing the basket a couple of times. Jim grabbed the basket and held it next to him.

"It looks like I can't do anything right—I can't even make a basket," Maurice mumbled as he threw the ear of corn into the basket.

"I know what you mean," Jim quietly replied.

Maurice continued down the row of corn pulling off the ears and tossing them to Jim. "She's right you know," Maurice said in a solemn voice.

Jim grunted in agreement as he bent over to pick up one of the ears of corn that had fallen from the basket.

"Jim, I'm tired of her constantly reminding me of the mess I caused. And then doing it in front of everyone here..." Maurice's words drifted off.

"Maurice, I'm not trying to make excuses for her but she is just scared and upset. Jenny did the same thing in front of Roger and Carolyn when we went over to their house."

"So you know how it feels?"

"Believe me, I do. Someone once told me that truth sometimes hurts—and it does."

Maurice grabbed Jim's empty basket and walked over to the string bean row and began to pull off the beans from the vine and toss them into the basket. "So what did you do Jim?" Maurice asked with his eyes still focused on his task.

"Forgave her—*and* myself." Jim answered as he bent over to pick up the beans along the ground that had not made their way into the basket.

* * * * *

"I see Jim is talking to Maurice," observed Joy. "I'm glad. I feel so bad about what I said."

"I know how you feel, Joy. I did the same thing to Jim last weekend."

Joy stopped and looked at Jenny with tears in her eyes. "Jenny, I really hurt him…and…I said it in front of everyone here."

"Joy, I hurt Jim in front of Roger and Carolyn, a couple we had just met. I blamed him for everything." Jenny pushed her basket ahead a few feet.

Joy was pulling carrots out of the ground as Jenny continued, "When I blamed Jim for all of our financial problems, Carolyn interrupted my blame rant and told me that our financial problems were just as much my fault as they were Jim's." Joy stopped and looked at Jenny with a confused look.

Jenny smiled at Joy. "That's the same look I gave Carolyn."

"So what did she mean by that?"

"Carolyn said that by not speaking up when the purchases were being made, I was condoning his actions. When she first said that, I didn't agree, because I knew that I had confronted Jim in the past with some of his purchases.

The Law Of The Seed

But then she made her point by asking if I had co-signed on any of our loans. Well, of course I had. And then Carolyn asked, 'Do you see that you have some responsibility in this and that makes you partially to blame?'"

"Ouch," replied Joy.

"Yah, it hurt. But she was right. The more I thought about what she said, the more I realized that I played a large part in our financial mess."

Jenny looked at Joy, "Roger and Carolyn showed me that it was both of us that got ourselves into this mess and together we need to work to get out. Blaming Jim was wrong, and it was not going to help the situation."

"Joy, you need to forgive Maurice and yourself."

* * * * *

Maurice caught Joy's eyes. As he did he mouthed the words, "I'm sorry". Joy at the same time mouthed the same words. Overcome by emotion, Joy raced to Maurice with tears streaming down her face. Maurice embraced Joy, wrapping his arms around her.

The rest of the group, observing what was unfolding, began to clap.

Two quick blasts of the tractor horn interrupted the moment. Hank was standing next to the trailers and was motioning everyone to come back to the farm chariot.

Baskets full of fresh picked vegetables were placed on the floor of the trailers. "Great job everyone. We are going to have a great feast today," commented Hank as he finished placing the last basket on the floor.

Turning towards the group, "In about four hours, at six o'clock, the farm chariot is going to pick you all up for the largest and best harvest celebration that you have ever participated in. We are going to have barbecue chicken and pork, vegetables and fresh baked pies. What you picked here is going to be eaten today. Before you guys walk back, I want to share a farmer's truth with you. Go ahead and take a seat where you are."

"A lot of farmers practice the Law of the Seed and understand the Harvest Principle and they are successful. Some of these farmers, even though they are financially successful, their personal lives are not."

"There is a farmer's truth that many cannot and will not accept and that is the Truth of Forgiveness. The farmer's truth of forgiveness gives a person the power to move on—to have a new beginning."

"I have seen farmers refuse to forgive another person for a wrong that they had done, even when the person has asked for forgiveness."

"Instead, these farmers will let the wrong eat away at them year after year. That is not living a successful life."

Hank held up a palm sized cross. "Our kids designed this cross, which is constructed out of nails. To me, this cross is the best symbol of forgiveness. I have it lying on my bedroom dresser as a reminder to forgive people and myself."

"Today, I watched two individuals forgive themselves and then I observed them as they forgave each other. I know that many of you saw it too."

"You all have plenty of time before the Harvest Celebration to talk and forgive. Let me challenge you as you walk back to the stables, to take that time to forgive yourself and forgive your spouse. Forgiveness clears the soul and allows you to move on."

The Law Of The Seed

"Oh, I almost forgot, the kids left this symbol for each of you in your rooms. May it remind you of the power of forgiveness."

"Alright, we will see you at six at the Harvest Celebration."

The tractor roared to life and off they went, leaving the group to themselves to walk back and talk.

15
The Harvest Celebration

Truth of Treasures and Time – Your focus should be on treasures that matter and that will last.

Then he said to them, "Watch out! Be on your guard against all kinds of greed; a man's life does not consist in the abundance of his possessions."
Luke 12:15

"All aboard, next stop Harvest Celebration," instructed Heather. "This is our next to last ride together and for your listening pleasure, Caleb and I have selected a blast from the past and we need your help. For those of you who can't sing, don't worry, you can do this song. Here goes."

As the farm chariot began to lurch forward the theme song from the The Andy Griffith Show played over the intercom. With the microphone still on, Heather did her best, as did the rest of the group, to whistle along.

The farm chariot pulled up beside a trail. "Folks, this is the closest that we can get. The Harvest Celebration is just through those trees. Just follow the trail."

The trail opened up to a grassy area where a large tent was set up in front of a beautiful lake. The lake had a small foot bridge across it that led to a board walk lining one half of the lake. Next to the tent was a huge barbecue pit where smoke could be seen pouring out. Under the tent, were

The Law Of The Seed

numerous white cloth covered tables and chairs, each one uniquely decorated with colorful flowers.

All of the Ripple Farms' staff members were there along with many other people that Jim and Jenny did not recognize. There were many kids all dressed up in coveralls, with red bandanas around their necks. Some of them were carrying trays of drinks. Jim estimated there were between 75 and 100 people.

"If everyone would find a seat, we would like to get started," sounded Camp Director Ray's voice through the speakers. As Jim and Jenny entered the tent area, they found each place setting had name cards. They discovered that their seats were toward the very front. Sitting across from them was a couple that appeared to be in their late thirties. They introduced themselves as Arlie and Cathy Mills.

Ray started the introductions. "I would like to personally welcome everyone here. It's great to see some old familiar faces—friends, family and past financial farmer trainees. Thank you for coming, as we celebrate the current graduating class of Financial Farmers."

"In just a minute, I'm going to dismiss all of the guys, section by section, to go and serve the ladies. For those that are visiting with us this evening, let me tell you why. Today our group of Financial Farmers had a friendly competition that the guys lost. The wager was that the loser would serve dinner to the winner. So tonight the ladies get to relax and enjoy their meal."

Just as Ray finished his announcement, a chorus of cheers arose from the ladies.

Ray waited until the cheering stopped. "Tonight, I have asked Arlie Mills, one of our past Financial Farmer graduates and a successful dairy farmer to bless our food and our time together. Arlie?" Ray handed him the microphone.

The Harvest Celebration

After the prayer was finished, the men rose in unison, and headed to the food tables to serve the ladies. The tables were filled with barbecue pork and chicken, steak, baked and mashed potatoes, green beans, corn, rolls and various types of salad. It was a feast. The men did their best to serve the winners, including Maurice, who managed to scrounge up a serving tray.

Carrying a single plate high above his head, he delivered it to Jenny, "Here you go my Ladyship, bon appétit."

To Jenny's surprise, the plate was piled high with every food offered and large enough to feed two people. "Why thank you kind Sir for being so generous. I shall enjoy this…for the next five days." The entire table laughed.

Just as the men sat down with their plates, Ray interrupted the meal with an announcement, "Go ahead and continue to eat and while you are doing so, we have a video to show, featuring all of our past and present Financial Farmers. Enjoy!"

The video was projected on a large screen that was hanging down from one corner of the tent. The video had names and dates underneath each of the pictures as they flashed across the screen to music. The video also showed the rehabbing of the stalls into rooms and the refurbishing of the barn. The forty minute video concluded with a quick time lapse of a garden growing—from seed to harvest.

"I'm very proud of all of you," commented Hank as he moved in front of the small podium up on the stage. "It's great to see so many familiar faces and to hear the exciting things that have taken place in your lives since you went through the Law of the Seed program."

"Instead of me sharing and tying things together from the lesson that you learned today, I have asked some of our graduates to share. These are true stories, coming from real

The Law Of The Seed

people, just like you. I know that you will be inspired as much as I have been."

"I have asked Steve and Laura to kick things off for us. As they make their way up here, let me briefly tell you about them. Steve and Laura were one of the first couples to go through our program. Steve is a successful landscape architect and Laura is also very successful as a real estate agent specializing in waterfront properties. When they came into the program they were close to half-a-million dollars in debt. Today—well, I will let them tell how you much debt they have. Farmers, please welcome Steve and Laura Adams."

Truth of Treasure and Time

The group warmly welcomed Steve and Laura to the stage. "Thank you so much for that welcome. Laura and I are especially honored to be here and share part of our lives with you."

"Fourteen weeks ago today, I was convicted. When Roger shared the story of the tractor and the barn, that hit home with me. You see, I was a tractor collector—a big time collector. I had a jet ski, a boat, a truck, two BMWs, a Harley, a nice large home with a pool and many other toys. All that stuff—those toys were going to decay over time. They were going to rust and become worthless."

"Now to some of my friends and neighbors, we were well off. In reality we were in debt—big time. We had very little in savings and hardly anything in retirement. The worst part of the whole thing is that I was absent from the lives of my children. The Farmer's Truth of Treasure and Time tells us to focus on living for things that will last. My family will last if I pass on to my kids sound teachings, values that will guide them, and share with them about a heavenly father who loves them."

"Life changed for me that day. I became a committed Financial Farmer. That day, Laura and I committed to become debt free in 24 months. I am glad to say that we are well on our way. I'm going to have Laura tell you what we're doing." Steve handed the microphone over to Laura.

"As Hank mentioned, we were close to $500,000 in debt when we attended The Law of the Seed weekend workshop. We decided to apply what we learned, and with the help of the workbook, we were able to reduce our debt to just around $200,000." Laura was interrupted by the gasps coming from the group.

"I know that it's hard to believe—but we've eliminated close to $300,000 of debt. And you know what's strange? It wasn't that hard. We just followed the steps of the Law of the Seed. We planned, prepared, planted, provided and protected our seed."

"I know we don't have a lot of time but I want to share a few things that we did. The biggest thing that we decided to do was downsize. Our home was nice but too big. We sold our home and walked away with $140,000. We bought another home which is much smaller but it's nice and in a very nice neighborhood. The neighborhood has a community pool, tennis courts and playground. It also was in the same school district, which meant that our kids wouldn't have to change schools and make new friends."

"The home cost us $249,000. We put down $100,000 and financed the rest. We used the majority of the $40,000, which was left over from the sale of the house, to pay off the truck, and the credit cards. We sold one of the BMWs at a loss and ended up paying the dealer about $3,500."

The Law Of The Seed

"We still have the boat and the older BMW to pay off. But we are well on our way to becoming debt free—and it feels good." Laura turned to Hank, who was standing just off of the stage, "Hank, thank you for allowing us to share, we are so grateful to you and the rest of the Ripple Farms' team."

Hank came up and stood beside them. "You are very welcome. Your story is so inspirational."

"Before you two take a seat, I have a few questions. Last night I gave an example of becoming debt free by developing a cash flow plan and taking the money saved from budgeting expenses to pay down debt. I used a couple from our current group as examples. Well, one of them asked a question if it could really be that simple. I didn't answer the question because I wanted them to discover the answer on their own. But since you two are here and Laura did say that it wasn't that hard, could you provide some insight about your cash flow plan?"

"Hank, I wanted to mention that but I forgot," replied Steve. "I should have stuck to my notes."

"Well, let me say that Laura and I never ever had a cash flow plan. And when we decided to plan and track all of our expenses, we were shocked at where our money was going. It really was embarrassing to see the money being wasted."

"A couple of examples—our yearly home expenses dropped by $12,000. Just by downsizing. Our electric dropped by $250 a month, we have no pool expenses now and our landscaping expenses were reduced by half. Our home insurance and property taxes also dropped significantly."

"We also stopped feeding our kids which saved us a lot of money—just kidding. But I will tell you that we stopped eating out as much. When we started tracking our expenses, we found that more than 75% of our food expenses were due to eating out."

"Laura mentioned that we are following the Law of the Seed, and I know today you shared and discussed the last two principles of the Law of the Seed, 'provide and protect'. I want to conclude by telling you how Laura and I are using those two principles for becoming debt free."

"Our harvest, the end result, is to be debt free and our seed is our money. Now to make sure that our seed of money does not dry up but continues to produce, both of us are still working hard at our jobs. This provides a paycheck—money to pay down debt."

"We also started taking some educational classes to enhance our skills. By continuing to work hard and by becoming more educated, we are protecting our job—our money seed. We are becoming more valuable to our companies and should there be layoffs, both Laura and I are better positioned to weather that storm."

"Oh, I almost forgot—to protect each other from using the money seed for other purposes, Laura and I have started using a simple ledger sheet to track our daily expenses. By doing this we can make sure that we are not spending more than we had planned for a particular expense, like eating out. And it's working!"

Hank wrapped his arms around Steve and Laura and hugged them. "I am so proud of you two. What a great job you are doing."

As Steve and Laura made their way off stage, they received a loud round of applause.

"Our next couple are real live farmers—dairy farmers. Together they run a dairy farm, milking around 400 cows twice a day, seven days a week, 365 days a year. It's hard

The Law Of The Seed

work. Arlie and Cathy were in the same group as Steve and Laura. As farmers, Arlie and Cathy had a good understanding of the Law of the Seed, but they struggled with something else."

"Please welcome Arlie and Cathy Mills."

The Truth of Ownership

Arlie and Cathy made their way up on stage to the applause of the group. Cathy spoke first. "Wow, what a blessing it is for us to be back here today." Cathy paused for a moment, looking behind her and then into the attentive audience. Speaking slowly and with sincerity, "Hank, Sue, Roger, Carolyn, Joe, Linda, Ray and Cindy, thank you for all that you do. You have touched our lives more than you will ever—."

Before Cathy could finish, the entire group immediately rose to their feet and recognized the whole staff. Jim also rose to his feet and enthusiastically clapped for the Ripple Farms' team. Looking around he observed both Hank and Roger wiping away tears. *They really are great men,* he thought.

Cathy waited until the clapping stopped and then continued. "When Arlie and I attended the program 3 ½ months ago, we didn't realize how much our lives would change as a result of that weekend."

"Although we knew the Law of the Seed principles, we were not diligent in applying them every day to our lives and to our business. When we returned home and started working through the workbook, things began to change. Our—*my* outlook changed. You see, what affected me, was not as much the Law of the Seed but the farmer's truths that go hand-in-hand with the Law of the Seed."

The Harvest Celebration

Arlie touched Cathy on the arm and whispered something to her. Cathy smiled at him and continued. "Arlie just reminded me that not all farmers are created equal and that most of us are what he calls, 'half farmers'. I know that sounds weird—let me explain that before I continue.

"For those of us that are married, our spouse is different. We each bring unique gifts, talents and skills to our marriage. We are, according to my wonderful husband, 'half farmers'. We are uniquely different, and together we become a *whole* financial farmer. Arlie has certain financial farmer strengths and I have other financial farmer strengths; when we combine those strengths, we become whole financial farmers."

"I say all that because, when we attended the camp, I was convicted about a lot of things. But there was one financial truth in particular that really got my attention, and it was not the same one that convicted Arlie. He already understood this truth and lived it."

"I am talking about the truth of ownership. This truth says that we are managers not owners of the things in our lives. In church, we say that we are stewards. I like manager, because I can relate with that term."

"Believe me, to really understand and believe that I am just a manager, took some time for me to accept. But over these last 3 ½ months, I have finally grasped that everything—and I mean *everything* belongs to God and I am his manager of what he has entrusted to me."

"If I could share one quick story—". Cathy looked at Arlie, who nodded his head for the go-ahead. "Well, about two months ago, our mower broke down. We had enough repair money to cover the $1,200 that was needed. But I thought we were wasting money and that we should purchase

The Law Of The Seed

a brand new mower for $8,400. We had close to $11,000 saved in our repair account."

Cathy suddenly stopped, stepped back and handed the microphone to Arlie. Cathy just stood there, watching Arlie, who was deliberately taking his time as he moved slowly to the front of the stage.

"I know what you're thinking," responded Arlie to the growing sound of whispers coming from the surprised group. "You are probably asking yourself, 'why did she stop?' There must be something wrong? Maybe she needs to go to the outhouse?'" The group laughed.

Truth of Understanding

"Well you are wrong and you are wrong. Cathy is fine, and she does not need to visit the ladies' room. You see, the story that she was sharing, involved me also. Before we tell you what we did, I just want to take a minute to tell you about another farmer's truth that really impacted me and it affected the outcome of our mower problem."

"When we were here, Hank shared the farmer's truth of understanding. The truth states that decisions based on wisdom, knowledge and having an understanding lead to success. Understanding is key."

"I know about dairy farming, I know cows. I have a solid knowledge of milk production but understanding the business of dairy farming is a different story. So after that weekend, when we diligently started applying the Law of the Seed to every facet of our dairy farming, I knew I needed to gain a deeper understanding of business finance. So, I started taking some college classes. Those classes are helping me develop a deeper appreciation and understanding of business finance."

The Harvest Celebration

"When Cathy and I were faced with repairing the mower or purchasing a new one, we decided not to do either one. We hired someone to start mowing."

"A friend of ours offered to mow our property for six months for free in exchange for our mower. After six months, he would charge us $400 a month. When Cathy and I started calculating all of our costs with mowing the property ourselves, taking into account our true operating costs, such as our time, fuel, and mower repairs, it was costing us close to $550 a month."

"So as good managers of what has been entrusted to us, we got out of the mowing business, which saved us money, and it allowed us to focus more on our dairy—a win-win."

"In closing, Cathy and I want to encourage you to stay the course. The Law of the Seed does work when you follow the steps and when you apply the farmer's truths. Thank you for allowing us to share."

The Law Of The Seed

16
The Bridge

Do what you can, with what you have, where you are.
Theodore Roosevelt
1858-1919, President, Explorer, Author, Soldier

Good intentions are not good enough... ultimately we are measured by our actions.
Source Unknown

All of the Ripple Farms' team joined Hank on stage. Camp Director Ray moved to the center, "We would like to recognize each and every one of you by awarding you with a Financial Farmer Certificate. We also have a little gift package that we call 'Seed Planter' that we want to give you. The 'Seed Planter' contains a DVD of your time with us, 100 business cards, a bumper sticker, a plaque and some packages of seeds. All of these are tools that you can use to spread the word with others about what you have learned here."

Ray called the group members up, one by one. Each person went through the line, shaking hands and receiving their certificate and gift package. Each person received a standing ovation along with loud whistles and cheers. As soon as the last person had been recognized, Ray motioned for everyone to sit down.

Ray handed Sue the microphone. "There are two more things that we want to share with you. The first is the puzzle—we need to finish the puzzle." Just then a tarp from behind the stage was dropped revealing the unfinished puzzle.

"Six pieces remain. Today you learned the last two principles of the Law of the Seed; 'Provide and Protect'." Sue held up the two puzzle pieces for everyone to see and walked over to the large framed puzzle and snapped them into place.

The picture within the puzzle began to take shape. To Jim and Jenny the bottom half of the puzzle looked like water.

Standing at the puzzle frame, Sue continued. "You also just learned some new 'Farmer's Truths'. The Truth of Treasure and Time says that our focus should not be on things that rust and rot but on treasure that matters and that will last." Sue added the piece to the puzzle.

Sue held up another piece that was labeled "Forgiveness". "Truth of Forgiveness is powerful. In order to move on in life, you must forgive others and yourself."

While Sue inserted the odd shaped piece, she continued talking. "Another truth that was shared just a few minutes ago was the Truth of Ownership. Whether you choose to accept this truth or not, the fact remains that we are charged to manage what has been entrusted to us and to make it grow for our heavenly owner."

"And the last piece that Arlie just talked about—the Truth of Understanding." Sue inserted the last piece and stepped away.

Everyone recognized the finished puzzle immediately. It was a beautiful picture of the very lake that they were sitting next to. Even the bridge was shown, located just above the center of the picture frame.

The Law Of The Seed

Looking closer at the bridge, the keystone was prominently displayed, having a different color and larger than the rest of the rocks that formed the bridge.

Directly under the keystone and on the surface of the water, the picture showed a small circle, with larger circles surrounding the first circle, all growing larger until they touched the banks of the lake. They were ripples.

As Jim and Jenny were looking over the completed puzzle, it began to pivot up towards the ceiling of the tent. Just then the lights turned off. Everything was completely dark. No one could see anything.

Suddenly a tiny light could be seen off in the distance, and then another. Slowly the entire bridge was outlined in white lights, a beautiful silhouette, against the dark void. The surface of the lake was like glass and the lights from the bridge reflected off of it, forming a second bridge.

Just as Jim, Jenny and the rest of group were admiring the bridge lights, more lights appeared along the water's edge, outlining the lake. It was breathtaking.

Jim and Jenny felt a tap on their shoulder and then someone whispered, "Follow me." Jim and Jenny did as instructed and disappeared into the darkness.

Jim and Jenny followed the dark figure out of the tent and along the tree line that bordered the lake. The figure stopped behind a large oak tree, which was large enough to hide the light from the flashlight as it was turned on.

Carolyn turned the flashlight on, pointing it towards the sky revealing Roger, the dark figure that Jim and Jenny had been following. "Sorry for taking you away from the festivities," whispered Roger. "But we need you two to help us with something."

"Of course we'll help," Jim answered curiously. "What do you want us to do?"

The Bridge

* * * * *

The stage, along with the entire tent area, began to light up, as Tiki torches were lit. The flame of the torches gave off a warm orange glow. Hank appeared just in front of the stage, careful so as not to block the view of the lake and the bridge.

"Our time with you is coming to an end. It has been a terrific weekend. Our prayer has been that you learned a lot, but more importantly that you will take what you have learned and apply it to your lives."

"We want to hear stories like the ones that were shared tonight from our past graduates. Maybe, just maybe, you will join us and share your story to a future financial farmer graduating class."

"Tomorrow, the *real* work begins. No, I'm not talking about your job, but I am talking about your job as a Financial Farmer. Over these last three days we have shared the foundation to having a successful financial life. Now it's time for you to build your financial home on that foundation."

"When you arrived at Ripple Farms, you received a box that was labeled, 'Financial Farming Kit'. In that kit was a notebook. That notebook is your guide for the next 6 weeks. Work through each section, one week at a time. If you're married, work on it together, this is a joint effort."

"By the sixth week, your financial life *will* be different. You will experience a peace about finances that you have probably not experienced since you became an adult—the Harvest Principle and the Law of the Seed work."

The Law Of The Seed

"Now, before you leave, we have one last thing that we want to share. If you could all look toward the bridge…"

At that moment, a large street light began to flicker as it was turned on at the bridge, slowly lighting up the bridge as the bulb grew warm, revealing Jim and Jenny who were standing alongside of Roger and Carolyn. On the railing of the bridge was a microphone, along with two large round rocks.

Roger took a step forward and began to speak. "This lake—this spot is very special to all of us at Ripple Farms. This is where Ripple Farms and our group got its name, and it is where 'The Law of the Seed' took root."

"A year-and-a-half ago, Carolyn and I never imagined that we would be helping to run a camp, much less meeting new and wonderful people each month. It has been a humbling experience for us." Roger paused for a moment and turned around and looked at Jim and Jenny.

Turning his attention back to the group sitting under the tent he continued. "Just a week ago we met a family and today we call them our friends. I have asked our new friends, Jim and Jenny Smith, to share something with you all." Roger took a small step back.

Jenny held on to Jim's hand as he began to speak. "Roger and Carolyn asked us to share what brought us to Ripple Farms." Jim shifted his weight to his other leg and clasped Jenny's hand a little harder. "I attribute us being here to three things—a kind gesture, a business card and a 'hope seed' that was planted."

"Like Roger said, 'it was a week ago' that we met. Roger had no idea that by his simple act of kindness toward my wife and two kids, he and Carolyn would impact our lives so much."

The Bridge

"Believe it or not, he paid for our groceries, perfect strangers, when my wife forgot her checkbook at home. He also gave her the 'Law of the Seed' business card, just like the one we received tonight. It was that simple business card that led me to go online to visit the website and see what this was all about."

"I sent Roger an email and then our families met. It was he and Carolyn that planted the 'hope seed' in us last weekend. You see we had lost hope. It wasn't luck that brought us together but rather God who planned it all. To God, we are grateful. And we are grateful to Roger and Carolyn and the entire team for opening up this farm and their lives to us. Our lives have been forever changed." Jim looked at Roger, signaling that he was done speaking.

Roger and Carolyn moved up to the railing and placed their hands on one of the large round rocks and pushed it into the water. The rock made a loud splash. The lake, which was once smooth like glass, was now full of ripples. Roger and Carolyn did not say anything, they just watched the water. Minutes passed. Roger motioned to Jim and Jenny.

Both Jim and Jenny moved to the railing and just like Roger and Carolyn, pushed the remaining rock into the water. It too made a splash that caused ripples to race across the lake.

"Our lives are like that rock. We can make a splash that produces ripples that can affect everyone that we come in contact with." Roger continued.

"This weekend our ripple was teaching you the Harvest Principle and the Law of the Seed. Our splash has positively affected the lives of Jim and Jenny. And others of you were positively affected by someone else's ripple and that is why you are here. For the ripples to continue, we need you to make a splash."

The Law Of The Seed

"Just as Jim and Jenny pushed their rock into the same pond as we did, I challenge you to make a splash with your life, causing ripples that will affect others as you come in contact with them. Share those business cards, display the bumper sticker and live a life of a successful Financial Farmer."

"By my actions and your actions, seeds of hope will be planted and together we will make a difference as Financial Farmers."

"Good night and God bless you."

17
The Ripple Effect

*What would you attempt to do
if you knew you would not fail?*
Robert Schuller
1926 – Present, Pastor, Author

"Mr. Smith, this is Norma from the front desk, I have a call for you on line three from your lovely wife."

"Thank you Norma," replied Jim who was just finishing reworking a spreadsheet for one of his clients.

Cradling the phone on his shoulder, Jim answered the phone, "Hi Jen, what's up?"

"I've got some good news for you, Honey. I was able to pay off another credit card today *and...* ," Jenny emphasized the word by dragging it out. "We were able to save $600 by combining our home and car insurance with the company that Maurice and Joy use."

"That's great, Jen! Good job."

"Thanks Honey. By the way, I have a favor to ask, if you don't mind."

"What is it?"

"I didn't get a chance to drop by Wal-Mart today to pick up our Friday night movie. Would you mind picking it up? I've already reserved it online. Also, we are a little short of milk and apple juice."

"Not a problem," replied Jim as he finished clicking 'save' on the Excel spreadsheet. "By the way, do we still

The Law Of The Seed

have some grocery money available for cake? You know, another debt paid off calls for a celebration."

"Yes, there's still some money left in the grocery budget. In fact, we will have some extra this month."

"Alright, I'll see you in about an hour. Love you."

"Love you too," replied Jenny.

Jim wrapped up a few things and within fifteen minutes was on his way to Wal-Mart. *What a way to start the weekend by shopping at Wal-Mart*, he thought. *At least I get a cake out of the trip.*

As Jim entered the store he noticed only one person in line at the video kiosk. Usually, the line is much longer. Jim decided to wait in line before getting the groceries. No sooner did he get in line than the person finished. *So far, so good. I may be home sooner than I thought.* Jim swiped his credit card and the kiosk dispensed the movie that Jenny had reserved online, "The Ultimate Gift" with James Garner and Brian Dennehy.

Grabbing the movie, Jim walked into the store. Quickly making his way around, he grabbed a gallon of milk, the apple juice and even found a chocolate cake on sale. Impressed at how quickly he found everything, Jim made a beeline for the cash register. All of them were busy. Jim selected one that only had a couple of people in it.

Jim reached the cash register, just in time. A person pulled just behind him with a full grocery cart. Scanning the magazines, he waited patiently as the cashier processed the lady in front of him.

"I'm sorry but this card is not working either," the cashier smugly replied, handing the card back to the young mother.

The Ripple Effect

Jim stopped reading the covers of the magazines and turned his attention to the young mother, as she fumbled through her purse.

"Just a minute," the mother replied to her son as he was tugging at her pant leg. "My checkbook should be in here – I'm not sure where I left it." Her voice began to strain.

Jim noticed that the amount was just under $20. *Not a big deal, they had extra in their grocery budget*, he thought. *I'll just go ahead and pay it. The poor lady could really use a break.*

Jim reached into his wallet and pulled out a $20 bill and handed it to the cashier, "This one is on me."

The young mother was a little startled. "No. Please, I can't take your money. We have money, I just can't find it. I must have left my checkbook at home."

Jim sensing her anxiety by the tone in her voice, tried to calm her down. "Hey, it's alright. This same thing happened to my wife about a month ago. Don't worry about it."

The young mother stopped fumbling through her purse and looked at Jim. "I really do appreciate it. "I'll send you a check as soon as I get home. Please, give me your address."

"No, it's alright. Really, this one is on me."

The mother insisted. "No, I want to pay you back. Please give me your address?"

Jim took out his wallet. Opening it up, he found a "Law of the Seed" business card. He quickly wrote his address on it and handed it to the lady, who was placing her son inside of the cart. "Thank you so much sir—"

"It's Jim. My name is Jim Smith. And you are very welcome."

Jim watched as the young mother left the store, understanding now how Jenny must have felt.

The Law Of The Seed

Paying the cashier, Jim headed to his car. Placing the items on the passenger seat, Jim paused for a moment and closed his eyes and whispered aloud, "Thank you Lord for giving me this opportunity to share and for being able to plant a seed of hope."

Another ripple started, another life affected.

A Final Word...

*If you always do
What you've always done
You'll always be
What you've always been*
Josh McDowell
1939 – Present, American Writer, Speaker

Jim and Jenny Smith experienced an unforgettable and life-changing weekend but their story doesn't stop there.

After the weekend retreat, Jim and Jenny began to faithfully work through *The Law of the Seed Financial Workbook*. They vowed to each other to become an example of what a successful Financial Farmer is and to share with others the principle of The Law of the Seed.

Just like Jim and Jenny, I want to encourage you to keep going. Don't stop now!

Becoming a successful Financial Farmer is challenging and requires more work and guidance than can be shared in this 160—page book. Take the next step and visit our website, www.TheLawoftheSeed.com. Here you will find additional resources, including the companion workbook, videos, and our monthly newsletter.

> Follow Jim and Jenny Online.
>
> Watch them as they share their experiences through exercises in the workbook.
>
> TheLawoftheSeed.com

The Law Of The Seed

In addition to the resources, you will be able to meet Jim and Jenny online and follow exactly what they did after their weekend stay at Ripple Farms. You will be able to see firsthand how they turned their financial lives around.

I look forward to hearing from you and to celebrating in your financial success.

-Ron-

Appendix

Law of the Seed
Plan + Prepare + Plant + Provide + Protect = Harvest

The Law of the Seed states: *The seed by itself cannot do anything, but by planning and preparing for the seed; planting the seed, providing and protecting the seed; the seed will grow to yield a harvest.*

The Harvest Principle
The seed is the future. Take care of the seed and the seed will take care of you.

Farmer's Truths

- Truth of Giving — When you share and give of yourself to help others, you will be refreshed and blessed.
- Truth of Attitude – Your attitude and acting with intention determines your success.
- Truth of Relationships — With many advisors your plans will succeed.
- Truth of Focus – When you focus on the right goals, you will succeed.
- Truth of Forgiveness — Forgiveness allows you and others to move on and start anew.
- Truth of Ownership – You are a manager not an owner of the things in your life.
- Truth of Treasures and Time – Your focus should be on treasures that matter and that will last.
- Truth of Understanding – Decisions based on wisdom, knowledge and having an understanding, lead to success.

The Law Of The Seed
Resources

We invite you to continue your experience with *The Law Of The Seed* at our website:

www.TheLawoftheSeed.com

The Law Of The Seed Financial Workbook
Companion workbook to help you become a successful Financial Farmer

Seed Talk
Video series to help you on your journey to become a successful Financial Farmer.

The Law Of The Seed Newsletter
Monthly newsletter full of tips and advice.

The Law Of The Seed Book
Purchase additional books to share with friends and family.

Plus many other resources to help you.

www.ingramcontent.com/pod-product-compliance
Lightning Source LLC
LaVergne TN
LVHW051600070426
835507LV00021B/2679